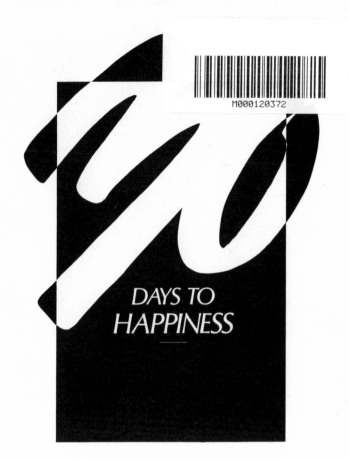

90
DAYS TO
HAPPINESS

To Penny —
So good to meet
you! Happiness!
Just hugs - Kristain

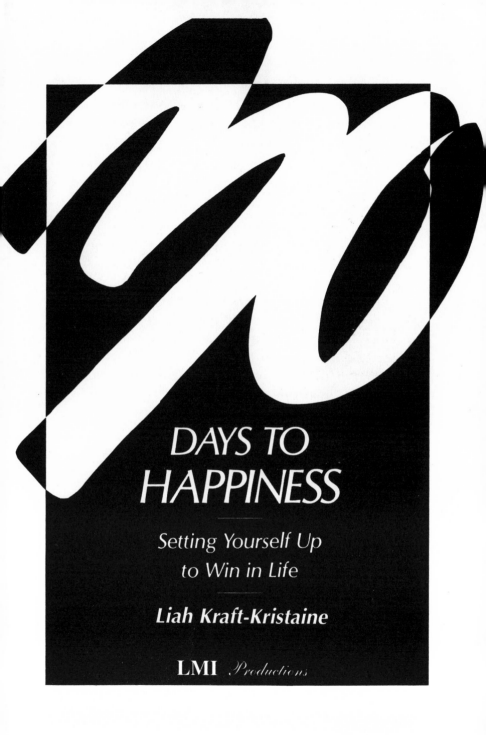

90
DAYS TO
HAPPINESS

Setting Yourself Up
to Win in Life

Liah Kraft-Kristaine

LMI *Productions*

This book is manufactured in the United State of America.
Cover art and text designed by Eismont Design. Published by
LMI Productions, a division of Life Mastery Institute
International, P.O. Box 150543, Nashville, Tennessee 37013.

Library of Congress Card Catalog Number 87-061158
Kraft-Kristaine, Liah

30 Days To Happiness

ISBN 1-878095-21-8

This book is dedicated
to those
who want to make the world a better place,
starting where it must begin:
a better place
FOR YOU.

ACKNOWLEDGMENTS

I want to thank the wise and wonderful friends who have helped me to grow over the past few years. Some of these friends I have never met, but only know through their books which, for periods of time, were my constant companions.

For changing my life and for inspiring this book, I wish to thank Shakti Gawain, Ruth Ross, Sondra Ray, Catherine Ponder, the Unity organization, U.S. Anderson, Ernest Holmes, Edgar Cayce, Patricia Hayes, John J. Falone, Ken Keyes, Jr., Dr. Joseph Murphy, Ann Wigmore, Jane Roberts, and, of course, Seth.

I give thanks to my personal friends and loved ones who have given me the continuing opportunity to learn and love every day. Your support and care has helped me hold fast to my path.

Finally, I acknowledge the creative power, both within and without, that has guided me to write this book. Absent that, nothing would be; with it, everything is possible.

CONTENTS

AUTHOR'S NOTE

*This book was written for you — a person who truly
wants to put more happiness in your life. I've written this
book because, during the past few years, I've learned
some powerful "secrets," known and used by some of the
world's most successful people. By using these ideas, I
have dramatically changed my life for the better! I want
to share them with you.*

*I was a confused and unhappy person several years ago. After
a failed marriage and the death of my beloved mother, I sank
into a pit of sadness and anger. I didn't like the feeling inside,
but didn't know how to break out of it. Then my wonderful
friend, Denise, quietly gave me a little book. It said that we are
responsible for everything that happens to us, whether
we realize it or not.*

*Somehow, I knew deep inside that statement was true.
But I didn't want to believe it. How could I? I felt like a
victim of forces beyond my control. The idea that I could
have created the turmoil made me furious!*

*After I picked up the book from the floor, I read on. I
learned that we have tools available for creating our lives
exactly the way we want them. We just have to learn
how to hoe and furrow with the tools, harnessing and
directing our power, instead of flinging them all over the
garden. So, if I had created my misery, I could also create
my joy? Absolutely, Yes!*

I read many more books and met some wonderful people over the next few years, harvesting kernels of wisdom. I used the ideas, but not consistently. I saw results, but they weren't consistent, either. It was a patchwork quilt. I decided to pull them all together for myself in a notebook, add my own thoughts, and work with them every day. My life improved so quickly, I was astounded!

That's why I wrote this book for you. To save you time and energy. For each message in this book, you can find volumes written. In other words, this is the tip of the iceberg, but it is also a cohesive whole — in capsule form.

If a particular area really captures your interest, great! Go on and read those volumes. You'll find some of my favorites listed at the end of this book.

If I could pull myself up out of darkness with these ideas, I know you, too, can find a pathway to joy. These messages are powerful. Even the words from one message have changed the lives of many people. It will change yours. And as you radiate with more happiness, someone will ask you how you did it. Then you'll share with them. The more candles we can light in this world, starting with ourselves, the brighter the world will be.

Happiness is not a luxury, but a daily essential.

Enjoy your Journey!

HOW TO USE THIS BOOK

This book is intended to give you a simple road map. Step by step, you will rediscover yourself and rediscover that happiness is your birthright. But you must want to learn, want to change, really want more happiness in your life.

Each day's exercise is set up in a similiar way. All you need to do is set aside ten minutes every day, preferably in the morning. Or find a few minutes here and there. Every moment spent with this book will add to your life.

Read the day's message. Then read it a second time, really concentrating on the message. Following the message is an exercise. It's very important that you do the exercises. Only with time will you realize how powerfully they affect your life.

You may feel compelled to re-read the day's message later in the day. Do it. The more times you think about the message, the more thoroughly it will become a part of you.

Take this book wherever you go. It has been published in a compact, portable size. Read it while you're waiting for the bus, sitting at a traffic light, anywhere you find a few moments.

We all make resolutions to improve the quality of our lives. We vow to quit smoking, we go on diets, we set up exercise programs. Why not embark on a program to become happier?

Maybe some of you have already tried various programs, and quit before completing because you didn't have time. With this book, you don't have to make a lot of time. Just let the ideas cross your mind during the day as often as you can — while you're at work, driving, cleaning the house. You don't have to stop your life to make progress. Work these ideas into your life. Every step you take accumulates into big rewards!

How do we get more happiness? A lot of people would say it's just the luck of the draw, that it just happens to us, a feeling triggered by events out of our control. That simply isn't true. This book shows you how happiness is within your control — totally. You can learn to have abundant happiness continuously.

Try this new way of thinking and living for the next thirty days. Change is a process. Start with one building block and work your way upward, like a stairway to the top of the hill. The more you use these thoughts, the faster you'll see the results, of course. But don't stop using it because you've only got a minute or two. Each effort made accumulates, and before long, you'll see a happier person in the mirror.

At the end of 30 days, these ideas will have become second nature to you. And so will the feelings of satisfaction, joy, and control over your life! The results will continue to blossom long after you've finished this book.

NOTE: Those of you with quick, curious minds will be tempted to read straight through this book after discovering the treasure it holds. Go ahead. But make sure you return to study each day in its turn, putting each message to use before going on to the next.

Change can't be spoon-fed. It comes from your own efforts, however much that might be. But you'll find you want to do more and more with the book. The exercises are fun to do! Very quickly, they become automatic and easy.

Change doesn't happen by mental learning alone. You must combine it with experience, so you'll also feel understanding of the ideas. A Chinese sage said: "No action, no knowledge." You've got to do it to know it.

Experts say it takes 30 days to form a new habit. Why not form a happiness habit? A habit of reaching for joy, for the best in yourself, stretching, growing, leaping to new heights.

A new person in 30 days! Healthier, more effective, and radiant! People around you will see the difference and love it. As you light up yourself, you'll light up the world around you.

Let this book guide you on a beautiful journey to your New Self.

YOU ARE NOW READY TO BEGIN!

SECTION I: Where You Are - The Present

DAY

WELCOME! Today you start off on an adventure that will change the entire course of your life! To change your life, you must get rid of old thoughts and accept some new ones. Open your thinking. Relax.

THE FIRST STEP: YOU MUST ABSORB THE GREATEST TRUTH. It is the foundation, the corner stone, the most important idea for you to know. You will feel the truth of it, at your deepest level. You will know:

- YOU CREATE YOUR LIFE WITH YOUR THOUGHTS
- ALL THOUGHT IS CREATIVE
- YOUR THOUGHTS MAKE THINGS HAPPEN

A single thought in your mind is the seed for everything you do, feel, say, or make. It's the beginning of everything. Thoughts are energetic kernels that explode into reality.

THOUGHTS CREATE FEELINGS. If you want to feel happy, change your thoughts. Depressed, angry, jealous, or sad feelings don't just magically appear; YOU CAUSE them with your negative thoughts.

Putting Your Thoughts on A Diet

KEEP YOUR THOUGHTS STEADIED ON WHAT YOU WANT to happen and how you want to feel. Do you want to feel better more of the time? Do you want to feel strong, joyful, in control of your life? Then stop thinking thoughts of failure, of weakness, of fear. Quit worrying.

YOU HAVE MORE CONTROL OVER YOUR THOUGHTS than over anything else in your life. Just as you pull weeds from your garden, you can remove negative thoughts. Just as you plant flowers, you can plant joyful thoughts in your mind.

- *CONTROL YOUR THOUGHTS, AND YOU CONTROL YOUR WORLD*

Thoughts create everything that happens to you. This is the truth:

- *THOUGHTS PRODUCE RESULTS IN YOUR LIFE*
- *YOU GET MORE OF WHATEVER YOU FOCUS YOUR THOUGHTS UPON AND*
- *WHATEVER YOU THINK ABOUT, FREQUENTLY AND INTENSELY, WILL HAPPEN IN YOUR LIFE SO*
- *YOU GET WHAT YOU FOCUS ON, EVEN IF YOU DON'T WANT IT*

DAY 2

If you use your mind to focus on lack of money, worry about not getting a job, or about getting sick, that's exactly what you WILL get.

Your thoughts go on working, even though you are no longer consciously thinking them. It's like a merry-go-round you've set in motion; it keeps turning until you forcefully stop it, or until it runs out of momentum.

You can start to change this momentum with even a single step in the right direction. That step may be simply to STOP focusing your thoughts on the negative. Just let them go! It's easier than you think. Being "realistic" doesn't demand focusing on a problem continuously. That's the worst thing you can do.

Some people are addicted to negative patterns just as others are addicted to alcohol. They actually argue for their "right" to continue making themselves miserable.

FORGET NEGATIVE MEMORIES! Reviewing and reliving them definitely causes more of the same problems to come to you!

WRITE A NEW LIFE SCRIPT for yourself now!

YOU HAVE GREAT POWER that must be used in the right way.

Putting Your Thoughts on A Diet

TODAY'S EXERCISE:

Re-read this message three times today. Your assignment for today, and for the entire thirty days, is to watch your thoughts.

Stop focusing on negative possibilities or negative past events.

As soon as a negative thought comes into your mind, LET IT GO. Gently put it out of your mind.

(This is YOUR DIET:) FOR THIRTY DAYS YOU WILL LIVE WITHOUT NEGATIVE THOUGHTS. You will focus only on the positive. You will think of all the beauty in your life, and all the beauty you want to bring into your life.

TODAY'S THOUGHT:

Drop negative thoughts like hot pans!

DAY 2

GOOD MORNING! Today you are going to see how controlling the words you speak can change your life. Never underestimate the power of words. You make your world with words, just as you do with your thoughts.

What is negative? Any statement of lack, limitation, failure, or unfulfillment. Look at the following statements:

"I'll never be able to learn that."

"I can't afford that."

"We'll probably always live from hand to mouth."

"I'm sure I'll be sick tomorrow, after staying out so late."

"I'll never find a job I like."

Do you think these statements are harmless? People talk about being realistic, as they defend setting themselves up for failure, poverty, illness and any number of other problems.

There is nothing realistic about saying such things as, "I never have enough money," or "I'm always sick." No one is "never" or "always" anything. Even saying, "This is going to be a rotten day," actually causes it to be rotten!

What You Say, You Get

When you focus on any negative situation, thinking and talking about it, you cause more of the same to happen to you. Many people use the term "self-fulfilling prophecy," but your spoken words aren't prophecy of a predestined event. Your spoken words set the event (bad or good) into action!

- YOUR WORDS ACTUALLY CAUSE THE EVENT TO HAPPEN

Have you ever noticed that when you tell someone you feel tired or ill, you begin to feel even worse? You would start to feel better almost immediately if you said, "I'm feeling better by the minute." Before you say anything, train yourself to ask,

- "DO I WANT THIS TO HAPPEN?"

The spiritual leaders of Egypt, India, Persia, China and Tibet have always taught the power of the spoken word. The Bible contains over two hundred references to the power of words such as, "Thou shalt decree a thing and it shall be established unto thee . . ." (Job 22:28)

DAY

Accept this truth:

- *WORDS ARE CREATIVE*
- *WHAT YOU SAY, YOU GET*

You have the power to turn a potentially wonderful situation in your life into failure by talking failure. ("I probably won't get that job," etc.) You also have the power to create incredibly good things. Some people fear "counting chickens before they hatch." They don't allow themselves to get excited over thoughts of a joyful future. The result: a life of mediocre and unsuccessful events.

The power of words is this: A positive statement of the good you want to experience is often all that is needed to turn the tide of events. It can swiftly and easily produce what you say.

Get excited about what you want! Talk about it with high expectation of it happening. But remember: if you can't do that at first, at the very least you must stop talking about things negatively. Clamp a hand over your mouth before you let yourself say that you'll be sick, poor, out of a job - or anything else that you don't want to have happen.

What You Say, You Get

TODAY'S EXERCISE:

For today and the remainder of these 30 Days to Happiness, you will rid yourself of negative statements and statements about things you don't want to experience. If a negative statement slips out of your mouth, immediately counteract it with a strong positive statement. For example, say: "No, I won't be sick tomorrow. I'm going to feel wonderful in the morning." Repeat aloud today's words (below) five times.

Remember:

- *SAY ONLY WHAT YOU WANT TO BE TRUE*

TODAY'S THOUGHT:

There is no such thing as a casual statement.

TODAY'S WORDS:

"My own words create miracles in my life."

DAY 3

GOOD MORNING! Have you ever given much thought to how you spend the first three minutes after you wake up? Surprisingly, those three minutes can be the most important of the day.

- *SET UP YOUR DAY WITH THIS "WAKING EXERCISE"*

1. *Immediately when you wake up in the morning, search for a thought that makes you smile. Then, smile!*

2. *Think of one or more people you love. Really let this feeling of love grow in you. Concentrate on it until you feel love filling you up like a warm, golden glow. Love activates!*

3. *Take five deep, slow breaths. Breathe in through your nose and out through your mouth. Don't hold your breath. With each inhalation, visualize a stream of white light coming in through the top of your head; with each exhalation, visualize the white light flowing down the length of your body and out through your toes.*

Starting Each Day

4. *See the white light as HEALTH, PEACE, JOY and LOVE. Visualize it running through your body like a stream of mountain water, cleansing your body and mind of any fear, negativity, impurities, and illness. See your body as perfect, vibrantly healthy, strong. Try to feel healthy and energetic, despite whatever may be going on with you. Then, see yourself feeling confident, poised, beautiful and capable. Do this until you feel great!*

5. *During this time, push away all thought of aches, pains and imperfections. Whatever you focus on, you'll get, so focus on health and energy. Imagining yourself being healthy and happy opens the door for health and happiness to come into your life.*

- *YOUR BODY'S NATURAL STATE IS EXHUBERANT HEALTH*
- *YOUR MIND'S NATURAL STATE IS HAPPINESS*
- *YOUR HEART'S NATURAL STATE IS LOVE*

DAY

3

6. Repeat to yourself five times: "HEALTH, ENERGY, HAPPINESS, LOVE." Feel the meaning of those words vibrate through you. The power of these positive words will increase your energy and transform you in only a minute or two. FOCUS on their meaning. Feel their meaning.

Super-charge yourself with this waking exercise. Get a fast start on the day. You'll be able to handle everything in your day more efficiently and happily, with far more confidence.

TODAY'S EXERCISE:

Repeat this waking exercise every single morning until the end of this 30 Days to Happiness. You'll want to continue it even after the 30 days are over.

In addition, anytime you think of it during the day, repeat to yourself: "HEALTH, ENERGY, HAPPINESS, LOVE." There's no better way to spend a few seconds.

Starting Each Day

Say today's words (below) aloud five times, morning, noon and night. On each day during this program, you must repeat the statement called "TODAY'S WORDS" in the same manner prescribed for today. It's extremely important that you say the words aloud. Repeat this procedure morning, noon and night.

Concentrate on the meaning of the words as you say them, and say them with authority. Fill up your room, your car, or all outdoors. Go where no one can hear you, if you're shy. Just make sure you say the words.

• *THEY WILL WORK MAGIC IN YOUR LIFE!*

TODAY'S THOUGHT:

Your personal power is activated with breath, love and energetic thoughts and words.

TODAY'S WORDS:

"Every day, in every way, my life is getting better and better!"

DAY

*GOOD MORNING! We all have times when we feel
particularly good about ourselves, when we really shine!
At these moments, your personal power has been
activated, and you feel alive, energetic, capable.*

- *THIS IS YOUR MOST NATURAL STATE OF BEING*

*But we have other moments, times when we feel at the
mercy of events, other people, illness, depression. You
can get control over those lows! You have tremendous
power! And you can learn to use it.*

*Every day, at every moment, you can choose to feel
strong. You are writing the script for your life every
minute. Start every day feeling great.*

- *YOU ARE IN CHARGE OF MAKING YOUR LIFE
  HAPPEN*

*Think of something you do that makes you feel full of
energy and life, an activity that makes you grin from ear
to ear: singing, dancing, running, reading, playing tennis,
doing yoga, talking to a favorite person, watching a
certain movie or actor, listening to motivational tapes. . . .
The possibilities are endless.*

Super-Charge Yourself!

Find your own "Super-Charger." Write it down. Find as many as you can. Discovering your "power button" is essential to getting in touch with yourself, your talents and abilities, and your undeveloped inclinations. Push that "power button" as early in your day as possible and whenever a down moment catches you.

- *SUPER-CHARGE YOUR PERSONAL POWER EVERY MORNING*

Fit one of your "Super-chargers" into your morning schedule and get energetic first thing! Then start your day: check off your errand list, go to a business meeting, greet your co-workers. You'll be amazed at how much more energetic, confident, and personally magnetic you are! You'll do things faster and think clearer. Everyone around you will notice and love it. It's contagious!

Take care of yourself. Be good to yourself. If that means getting up a little earlier so you can get in 20 minutes of singing, painting or exercising, do it.

DAY

Other side benefits can result. For example, you may think you're unhappy with your job because you don't seem to have a say about things. After activating your power button in the morning before going to that office, you'll be more cheerful, you'll feel better about yourself, and you'll be more confident about offering suggestions.

When we feel powerless, we think bad things are happening to us. That kind of thinking can make you feel helpless.

- *GIVE UP BEING HELPLESS*
- *GRAB HOLD OF YOUR LIFE*
- *PUT YOUR BEST SELF OUT THERE*
- *GET EXCITED*
- *GET STRONG*
- *REV YOURSELF UP*

You're already wonderful. Let yourself believe it. There's nothing egotistical in feeling great about yourself. Confidence is essential for health. Let your full-blown self shine.

Super-Charge Yourself!

Smile at yourself in the mirror. Turn on music in the morning. Laugh, even if you're alone. Fill up your world with yourself. Work will be more fun, play will be more rewarding, relationships will improve.

TODAY'S EXERCISE:

Write a list of activities that super-charge you. For the rest of these 30 days do whatever makes you super-charged every morning. Do not skip a day, not even on the weekends. Record an "A" on your chart (in the back of this book) when you've done the super-charger for that day. Notice how you feel in the hours that follow. You'll newly discover yourself. In just 3-5 days, you'll see changes all around you!

TODAY'S THOUGHT:

Be all you can be at every moment.

TODAY'S WORDS:

"I am bursting with energy and light."

DAY 5

GOOD MORNING! Do you give yourself enough love? Or do you fear that approving of yourself or accepting praise is egotistical?

- LOVING YOURSELF IS NECESSARY FOR GROWTH AND HEALTH

High self-esteem is not being egotistical. High self-esteem is being gentle with yourself, believing in your own goodness, feeling that you deserve the best.

Healthy self-confidence is attractive, it radiates from you, it attracts good things to you, and it's preventive medicine. Where do you kick yourself? Do you tell yourself that you're dumb or ugly or fat or undeserving?

People with low self-esteem not only hurt themselves, but they hurt everyone around them. If you don't feel worthy of love for yourself, you may resent giving it to others and may even try to make others feel bad about themselves. What a sorry state! Give yourself a lot of love, and you have a lot to spread around!

Loving Yourself

Wherever negative feelings came from in your life — from critical parents, teachers or peers — does not matter. Getting stuck in blame stops your growth. Forgive and leave it behind. Don't dwell on the ways you think you've been wronged.

- *BE A LOVING PARENT TO YOURSELF*

You are the creator of your life now. You are your own parent now. What matters is what you tell yourself.

Stop the negative self-talk — that chatter going on in your head day and night. Be constantly nurturing, encouraging, forgiving and supportive of yourself. You make a better world when you love yourself. You deserve it. You have a right to be here and to be the best you can be!

- *PEOPLE WILL TREAT YOU THE WAY YOU TREAT YOURSELF*

Don't talk in a degrading way about yourself and expect someone to come to the rescue. People generally will believe what you tell them through your words, actions and body language. Don't underdog yourself; stand straight, speak clearly, look straight into the eyes of your listener.

DAY **5**

Others are drawn to those who have self-respect. Yet some people are "poor-me'ers." Subconsciously, they want sympathy. And they may, indeed, get it. But at what price? They have traded their personal power for sympathy.

Don't look on the outside world for approval; buoy yourself up with your own approval. Don't expect to be rescued.

• *BE YOUR OWN "WHITE KNIGHT"*

TODAY'S EXERCISE:

DEVELOP HEALTHY SELF-LOVE.

Here are some ways to do that:

   1. *Give yourself what you want; feel that you deserve it.*

   2. *Have confidence in your abilities.*

   3. *Praise yourself verbally to yourself.*

   4. *Allow others to love you and praise you.*

   5. *Trust yourself and your instincts.*

   6. *Love your body and admire your beauty.*

Loving Yourself

7. *Reward yourself, never punish yourself.*

8. *Turn all negative "self-talk" into positive "self-talk."*

9. *Believe you can learn anything.*

10. *Look your best, present yourself with pride.*

11. *Don't compare yourself to others.*

12. *Have a kindly sense of humor about yourself.*

13. *Write a list of your abilities and accomplishments.*

Make your list today. Continue to work on self-love.

TODAY'S THOUGHT:

Self-respect attracts the best.

TODAY'S WORDS:

"My life is important. I treat myself the way I want others to treat me."

DAY 6

GOOD MORNING! Did you use the waking method this morning? Good! You'll better understand today's message.

- *VIVID IMAGINATION IS THE MOST IMPORTANT TOOL YOU POSSESS.*

You use your imagination every waking moment. However, many people use this ability for negative imaginings: fear and worry. Cultivating this innate talent for consistent positive use will be the most important step in your life.

Vivid imagining is called visualizing. Visualizing is focusing on a future event so completely that you can see and feel how it will be. The more intensely you experience the picture, the more likely it is for that vision to occur in reality. Using your imagination this way will actually create those events in your life.

If you think about a possible happy event, you feel more energetic, lighter; if you think about a possible negative event, your stomach may knot up. So, with imagination, you feel a possible future event as if it were happening right now!

- *VISUALIZATION IS A REHEARSAL FOR THE FUTURE*

Seeing Your Future

Remember: You already use this ability all the time. But too often this talent is used unconsciously, in ways that are harmful to you.

Let's say you have to give a talk to a group of people in a few days, and you're already getting butterflies. You've thought about standing before the audience, your voice quivering, your knees shaking, forgetting the words of your speech. By letting such imaginings into your mind, you're rehearsing for failure.

Instead, try using your imagination to see yourself delivering your talk to an appreciative audience and experiencing (this is important) confidence and ease.

Right now, think of something you're dreading today, fearing it will go wrong.

Take a few slow deep breaths. Now, see yourself going through whatever you have to do, doing it well, feeling calm, confident, and happy. See those involved believing in you and respecting you. Imagine everything going right.

If this is difficult to do, and you experience that ball of fear starting in your stomach, relax, take a couple of slow breaths, and start again.

DAY **6**

Work at this process until you can see yourself being successful all the way through whatever you have to do. As soon as you can do that, repeat the visualization immediately. It's like jumping off the high dive. When you finally succeed in doing it, do it again right away.

If, no matter what you do, you still can't see and feel a positive outcome, stop thinking about it. Don't spend another moment investing your negative imaginings with more mind fuel. Worry is negative visualization. Every time you run the failure scene through your mind, you hurt yourself and others.

- *EVERY TIME YOU VISUALIZE SUCCESS, SUCCESS BECOMES MORE LIKELY*

TODAY'S EXERCISE:
Every morning, think of what you have to do for the day. If any task causes a negative reaction in you, work with yourself until you can "see" a successful outcome.

Seeing Your Future

*USE VISUALIZATION TO CREATE SUCCESS IN ALL
AREAS OF YOUR LIFE: more income, a beautiful house,
a happy relationship. The more regularly and consistently
you focus on what you want, the more you actually
attract your desire into your life. Each time you visualize
brings it closer to you.*

VERY IMPORTANT:

- *EXPERIENCE WHAT YOU WILL FEEL WHEN YOU
  HAVE WHAT YOU WANT*
- *LET YOUR ENTIRE BEING FILL UP WITH THE RUSH
  OF POSITIVE EMOTION AND EXCITEMENT*

TODAY'S THOUGHT:

- *YOU CAN DO ANYTHING YOU BELIEVE YOU CAN*
- *BELIEF COMES BY VISUALIZING SUCCESS OVER
  AND OVER*
- *REHEARSE FOR YOUR SUCCESS!*

TODAY'S WORDS:
"I CAN CREATE MY LIFE WITH MY THOUGHTS!"

DAY 7

GOOD MORNING! Today you're going to see how affirmations can change your life. What is an affirmation?

In general, an affirmation is a positive statement about yourself or your life. It's a statement that directs your life to be exactly the way you want it. An affirmation is a way of shouting "YES!" to abundant life, to growth, to getting rid of blocks inside you.

- *AFFIRMATION — COURAGE TO TAKE A STAND ON THE FUTURE*

An affirmation is not a wish; wishing expresses doubt. To affirm is to "make firm," to make a statement a solid reality. Affirmations are in the present tense: a statement of firmness and belief that a desired condition exists now.

Examples: "I am now slender."

"Money is now flowing to me easily."

"My project is already successful."

"I feel great! I'm full of energy."

Each time you say an affirmation you've designed for yourself, you'll feel a pull of energy inside. The more you say it, the more you believe in it.

Magic Words:
Affirmations

*All day long, words flow through your mind. The
"self-talk" is endless. If all of us did positive, empowering
"self-talk," there would be no need for a book like this.
But the truth is, many people feed themselves negative,
limiting messages all the time: "People don't like me."
"I'm not smart enough." "Men aren't attracted to me." "I
can't do it."*

*Some of your negative messages have become so
habitual, you aren't aware of them. On a basic level,
you've brainwashed yourself. Those negative statements
affect everything you do.*

*Like a boat motor with weeds tangled in its propeller,
your ability to live to the fullest is choked by the
negatives. Affirmations help you get rid of the negatives
and get back to full power.*

- *YOU MUST COUNTERACT YEARS OF LIMITING
  THOUGHTS*

*How do you get out of the mire? The same way you got
stuck in the negatives: by repeating a message to
yourself over and over.*

DAY *7*

Affirming is not wishing; it's making a statement that an area of your life is now exactly as you want it. For example, if you need money, you won't say "I wish I had more money." You will say it this way: "I now have all the money I need and want." You will eventually learn to believe in your affirmation. You'll get excited. Then, the magic starts!

- *WHAT YOU BELIEVE, YOU WILL GET*
- *YOU CAN CHANGE YOUR LIFE RIGHT NOW BY CHANGING YOUR BELIEFS*

An affirmation is a positive message you impress on your mind. Frequent repetition activates your thoughts in a new way, and at the same time, erases the old programming. Continued repetition will produce permanent desirable changes in your life!

A powerful affirmation can produce results overnight. But in general, results appear after at least three days of strong affirmations. Some other affirmations take longer.

The more intensely you focus on your words, the more quickly you'll see results. But in every case, if you work on a specific affirmation every day for 30 days, tremendous change will happen.

Magic Words: Affirmations

- AFFIRMATIONS WORK MAGIC

TODAY'S EXERCISE:

Start using affirmations today. Choose one area in your life you want to change. Create a simple, short statement. Work with it until it says exactly what you want. Some affirmations will make you a little uncomfortable. That's good! You're really working on that old programming.

Find a time when you're alone and calm. Focus on the one simple statement that you have chosen. Then, for five minutes at the most, say aloud (and write, if you have time) your affirmations, twenty times for each one. Repetition is key.

Feel the statement in as many ways as you can — emotionally, mentally, physically. Really zero in on it and focus your thoughts. It's the most productive time you'll spend all day. Do it in a relaxed way, without strain. Then let it go, trusting that your intentions are now happening.

TODAY'S THOUGHT:

An intense thought always becomes reality.

TODAY'S WORDS:

"My words are powerful; they change my life."

DAY

GOOD MORNING! Now that you've started doing affirmations to clear up difficult areas in your life, you've probably noticed some negative reactions from yourself.

That's only natural. You've been programming yourself negatively for a long time. When you try to tell yourself an opposite, positive statement, it might be hard to accept — at first. After all, if you believe your new, positive words, that's like admitting you were wrong all this time! And that's pretty tough for some people.

But what's being a little wrong compared to opening up a whole new life for yourself?

Welcome these reactions from yourself. Although they're negative, don't shy away from them. Examine them, so you can release yourself from past barriers. They're great feedback!

Negative reactions show you:

1. Your hidden barriers,

2. Your negative beliefs,

3. How you should modify your chosen affirmation.

Affirmation Feedback

Remember that your old "programming," although limiting and harmful, is comfortable for you. Habits are comfortable, even bad ones. You may have to push yourself a little to stay with the new programming, but it's worth it!

Try this exercise for the first few days as you work on an unfulfilling area in your life. Write your affirmation at the top of a sheet of paper. On the next line, write down whatever you feel about the statement. Continue to write and respond until all your objections have surfaced. You will learn a great deal from your responses.

Do this for as many days as it takes until your negative responses diminish. At that point, you have begun to re-program yourself without interference. An example follows:

Tim was really down on life. He couldn't seem to break out of the earning/spending cycle enough to save any money to go back to school or to save money for a down-payment on a small house.

He wrote his affirmation and responses this way:

I now can make a lot of money.
That's a laugh.
I now can make a lot of money.

I always have to struggle.
I now can make a lot of money.
My dad always had to struggle; it's the same way for me.
I now can make a lot of money.
Of course, I've had more advantages than my dad.
I now can make a lot of money.
Yeah, but if I do, somebody will steal it, so why bother?
I now can make a lot of money.
Some people keep it. Why not me?
I now can make a lot of money.
Maybe I deserve to have a little money, too.
I now can make a lot of money.
My dad never felt he could. Maybe I can have a different
  life.
I now can make a lot of money.
Why not? It's possible, isn't it?
Anything's possible.

NEW AFFIRMATION:

I, Tim, now deserve to make and KEEP a lot of money.

Tim found out in this exercise that he was afraid to do
better than his father, and that these thoughts were
limiting him. He changed his affirmation so he could
focus on what his real barrier was: feeling undeserving.

Affirmation Feedback

Tim also learned that, subconsciously, he was afraid that if he somehow did save money, it would be taken from him. Very possibly, that hidden belief prevented him from doing his best or looking for the right jobs. Tim's beliefs were sabotaging him! Are yours?

TODAY'S EXERCISE:
Work on just one problem area in your life from now until the end of these 30 days. Use this feedback method until you don't need it any longer. At the end of this time, choose another area and work out an affirmation. Keep doing this until your life is what you want it to be.

TODAY'S THOUGHT:
Shine light on the shadows in your life.

TODAY'S WORDS:
"With each affirmation, my life gets better."

DAY 9

GOOD MORNING! Today you're going to get yourself out of slavery — a slavery to which you have chained yourself.

Every day, a lot of energy is spent worrying about and avoiding situations. You may not even be aware of it. We all have obvious fears, and fears we've hidden from ourselves.

For example, you may have a fear of heights, fear of a certain person, or fear of some aspect of your job. You may have fears that are less specific: a fear of being robbed, becoming impoverished and dependent, or even a fear of living.

Get rid of those fears! Confront the specific fears. Release the worry of floating, non-specific fears. Affirm that only good will come into your life. Say your affirmation over and over.

"ONLY GOOD THINGS COME INTO MY LIFE NOW."

Fear is based on the assumption that we don't have power over our lives. It springs from a lack of trust in the good in life, and the good in ourselves.

Fear shrinks your power. It causes immobility. For example, people become constricted and miserly when they don't trust that more money will flow in; they

Banish Fear

become hard with envy when they don't trust that opportunity and jobs abound for everyone, and that opportunity will come to them. Those negative thoughts must be counteracted by persistent affirmations of confidence and assurance.

But there's an even more important reason for banishing fear.

- *FEAR ATTRACTS THE THING FEARED*

Your own fears bring into your life scarcity, accidents, robberies, lack of opportunity and other unhappy events. A fear of being mugged can actually attract that occurrence! Fear can even attract the illness you think and talk about.

REMEMBER: We are all magnets. We attract whatever we focus on.

Don't clip articles about cancer, don't sit and endlessly discuss illness, robberies, accidents and bad luck, don't worry about every food you eat. Concentrate instead on everything going well. Get a clear mental picture of it. Stop expecting something to go wrong. We get what we expect!

DAY **9**

- *FEAR IS FAITH THAT BAD IS MORE LIKELY THAN GOOD*
- *FEAR IS USING FAITH NEGATIVELY*
- *FREE YOURSELF FROM FEAR*
- *LIVE WITH JOYOUS ANTICIPATION OF EVERYTHING GOOD HAPPENING*

TODAY'S EXERCISE:

Only you can free yourself from your fears. Start becoming aware of what you fear. Stop yourself when you find that you're thinking or talking about it.

Become aware of the "fear-talk" around you. Stop listening to it. You can try to explain to others why you don't care to discuss those things, but they may not understand. Don't push them. When they become ready, they'll pick up a book like this. Don't be evangelistic.

But it can be very helpful to find a friend with whom you can discuss these ideas. You can gently coach each other whenever you slip back into the old ways of talking and thinking.

Banish Fear

HOW TO DEAL WITH FEAR:

1. Specify your fear. As long as the fear remains unclear, it continues to have power over you.

2. Ask yourself what's the worst that could happen. Not only is the worst hardly likely to occur, but the answer might make you laugh!

3. Don't suppress your fear. Feel it. Talk about your fear objectively. Don't just stuff it away and pretend it doesn't exist. The amazing thing is this: when you study it and feel it, the fear disappears.

4. Create an affirmation that helps you. Make it specific.

Example: "My possessions and my body are completely safe."

TODAY'S THOUGHT:

You are as safe as you allow yourself to be.

TODAY'S WORDS:

"Only good comes to me. I have nothing to fear."

DAY 10

GOOD MORNING! Are you looking forward to this day with high anticipation? Or are you dreading it?

You can shape your entire day each morning by setting aside a few moments to visualize everything in your day going right. You'll feel terrific mentally, emotionally and physically.

Most important, it will help you remember that you're in control of your life. Sometimes, in the rush of having too much to do, we forget that basic truth. We rush this way and that, feeling pulled and pushed, anything but in control of the direction we're taking.

It's amazing how setting up a little routine in your mind can make all the difference in the way you feel.

Every morning, after you go through the waking up routine, do the following steps, in whatever order is comfortable for you:

1. Read from this book and do the assignment.

2. Do your affirmations.

Set Up A Winning Day

3. Give thanks for the day, for your health, for life.

4. Make a list of goals that you hope to achieve for the day.

5. Visualize accomplishing each goal in the best way.

6. Write a note of thanks that you've reached your goals.

7. Super-Charge yourself! (Day Four)

8. Say the following affirmation to yourself:

"I FEEL WONDERFUL! I FEEL FULL OF ENERGY!

TODAY WILL GO EXACTLY AS I WANT IT."

Say the affirmation at least ten times, aloud if possible, until you feel energy beginning to run through you and you find yourself smiling. Breathe deeply at the same time.

Your morning routine has taken very little time and you've saved yourself hours of frustration.

Happiness, contentment and peace come from defining what you want and telling yourself that you'll get there. Routinely writing your goals, whether morning or night, gives you a firm sense of direction.

And more than that: magic happens when you write things down. Goals seem to be met just because you've written them.

DAY 10

But you need to do this frequently in order to stay in touch with your changing self. At least once a week, review your goals. Find out what you truly want now, and what past desires you've outgrown. You waste energy and time in frustration over things that, deep down, you really wouldn't give your time and energy to work for.

To accomplish anything, you must have a strong desire. Real desire is intense and powerful; it can carry you forward, it can set up positive reactions in people around you, it actually seems to create the right timing and circumstances in which you can accomplish your desires easily and quickly.

Of the millions of things people say they want to do, very few have strong enough desire to set up goals and carry through. Yet, they're content to sit around and gripe about their lives. These people feel helpless, unable to control their lives. Don't be one of them!

• WE ALL CONTROL OUR LIVES; MOST PEOPLE JUST DON'T REALIZE IT

When you meet someone who's really going places in the world, that person seems radiant with a desire for the highest and best in life. He or she has learned to use the innate power available to all of us.

Set Up A Winning Day

TODAY'S EXERCISE:

Refer back to this Day until the daily routine becomes second nature to you.

A cautionary note: Be honest with yourself when you write out your desires and goals. Don't write what you think someone else wants for you, or what you think you should want. If you want happy results, your goals must be in harmony with your inner promptings. You must feel a sense of peacefulness and rightness.

TODAY'S THOUGHT:

Give thanks in advance for achieving your goals. Your trust gives more energy to your focus.

TODAY'S WORDS:

"I now reach my goals easily and swiftly."

SECTION II: You and Others - Reflections on the World

DAY 11

GOOD MORNING! Know this: You have tremendous personal power. You can do and be anything and have anything that you can clearly visualize and believe. You have total freedom of choice. This is the most important truth to know. At this point in this book, you are realizing these truths more and more.

You know now that you are responsible for everything that happens in your life. Every day you see that more clearly.

So now you must be warned of what could be a tremendous stumbling block on the path of having your life exactly as you want it: blame.

- *BLAME ROBS YOU OF YOUR POWER*
- *BLAME KEEPS YOU STUCK IN THE SITUATION*
- *BLAME BLINDS YOU TO THE LESSON TO BE LEARNED*
- *BLAME MAKES YOU THE HELPLESS "VICTIM"*
- *BLAME IS THE LOSER'S COP-OUT*
- *BLAME IS NEVER THE ANSWER*

Blame: The Crippler

It's simple: You either take responsibility for your life, or you play the victim of people, events and the world.

Every moment you face the choice of being a winner or a loser. A loser feels powerless. He'll claim that other people have luck, get all the breaks, or have good timing. Even when he does well, he'll shrug his shoulders and call it luck, and thereby diminish himself, his ability, and his personal power.

- *YOUR POWER COMES FROM SEEING YOUR CONTRIBUTION IN EVERY SITUATION IN YOUR LIFE*

The reward for taking responsibility is that we get to shape our lives. But it also requires courage to see what we did that wasn't what we wanted and to use that information to make changes for the future. The loser won't take that responsibility.

Living fully and growing requires that we see how we've contributed to every situation in our lives. That contribution might be negative or positive words, thoughts or beliefs.

We have a right to feel proud of the positive aspects of our lives, but we also have a responsibility to take care of the negative aspects and make them better.

DAY **11**

Blaming a spouse for your bad marriage, a mother for your lack of confidence, or a fifth grade teacher for your loss of interest in art, for examples, are all ways of being a loser. By blaming those people, you're actually saying that you're helpless. By doing that, you short-circuit your own power. You must take responsibility for all of your life, not just some of it.

Most blaming involves a payoff. That payoff might be to look better to our bosses or friends, or perhaps to escape punishment, or to get sympathy from others for our bad luck. Under all of these payoffs is a desire to avoid changing aspects of yourself that need to grow.

But know this:

* *YOU ALWAYS TRADE YOUR OWN POWER FOR THE PAYOFF AND THAT TRADE IS ALWAYS A TERRIBLE BARGAIN*

You may convince others that you're at the mercy of circumstances, but at the same time, you've convinced yourself. You lose your self-respect and your belief that you have the power to change each and every aspect of your life.

Blame: The Crippler

TODAY'S EXERCISE:

Make every effort to rid your thoughts and speech of blame. Notice how you go through your day, and how frequently you're tempted to blame people and circumstances for your discomfort. Accept responsibility for all of it today — from a flat tire to being late to getting promoted. It is vitally important to see our role, and to know that since you created the bad, you can also create what's good. From now until the end of this book, wipe blame out of your life.

TODAY'S THOUGHT:

Even good excuses rob power and energy.

TODAY'S WORDS:

"The more responsibility I accept, the more power and self-esteem I have."

DAY 12

GOOD MORNING! Do you walk around with your past tripping you up like a pair of pants around your ankles? Or do you know that all you need is to step up and out into a better future?

- *YOUR PAST DOES NOT HAVE TO PREDICT YOUR FUTURE*

Everything, every single thing in your life, can be changed for the better right now. You have the ability to choose what you want for your life and visualize yourself having it. It doesn't matter if your goal doesn't seem probable, based on the past. You can have it, if you believe it!

You will have it, if you will let go of any and all limiting memories of the past. Do not focus on the failures. It only brings on more of the same. Focus on the happiest times, the wins, the rushes of joy! Unlimited possibility awaits you, but you must believe it and concentrate on it.

- *THE PAST DOES NOT SET UP THE FUTURE*
- *YOUR PRESENT THOUGHTS SET UP THE FUTURE*

Letting Go Of The past

Don't be afraid of your past. It can't hurt you. Forget the failures and fears. Don't limit your thoughts based on what was possible before. The past has no power.

- *YOU ARE THE SOURCE OF POWER*
- *YOUR THOUGHTS, WORDS, IMAGINATION AND BELIEFS ARE YOUR POWER*

Visualize them churning and foaming together, creating more and more energy until, finally, they erupt like a geyser shooting steam and white foam high into the air. That's the kind of power you possess to create your future.

- *YOUR MOST POTENT POWER TO CREATE YOUR LIFE IS IN THIS MOMENT*
- *YOU ARE A NEW PERSON EVERY MINUTE*

You change every minute. The person you were five years ago is very different from the person you are now. It may be comforting for us to cling to our old definitions of ourselves, but how ridiculous to do that, if old definitions are limiting. Weed out the weakening statements. Focus on the strengthening ones.

DAY **12**

Dare yourself to start out fresh every day. Do something small that's different, so you can see how easy it will be to change something bigger.

Keep letting go of the past. Let go of the negative definitions of yourself, the anger, the jealousy, the envy, the blame, the resentment. Let go of the negative thoughts. Life flows. Flow with it.

Clean up problems as you go along. Problems never go away by themselves. Take care of all minor and major sources of irritation. If you don't, they'll come back to haunt you, and you'll be put on the defensive. Take the initiative first!

- *IMAGINE YOUR LIFE EXACTLY AS YOU WANT IT*
- *EXPECT A MIRACLE*

Yes, expect one! The past has no power over the future. Keep reminding yourself. Only your belief that the past dictates the future will keep you bound.

Letting Go Of The past

TODAY'S EXERCISE:

Push out the limits of your thinking in every area of your life today. Maybe it won't take you an hour to do that report, even though it has before; maybe you won't have friction with that co-worker today; maybe your number will be chosen, even though it never has been; maybe your day will be exactly the way you want it even though it never has been before.

There's no place for statements such as: "But it's always been that way . . . ," or "But there's no chance that could happen. . . ." Notice today how often and in how many areas of your life you put limitations on what wonderful things could happen to you. Then get free of those statements.

TODAY'S THOUGHT:

The past has no power, unless you believe it.

TODAY'S WORDS:

"I am willing to risk giving up all I have been, for what I can become."

DAY 13

GOOD MORNING! Imagine this: we are all like powerful magnets. Every day, every minute, we radiate and we attract. Our thoughts determine whether we draw the positive or the negative.

Have you ever noticed how some people seem to radiate confidence and success? They step into a room, and without a word, everyone is drawn to the good energy around that person. Positive thoughts act in exactly the same way.

On the other hand, you know people who seem to have the worst of luck. Whatever they do, it never turns out right for them. Eventually, you can see failure written in their postures, their expressions, their words. You probably shake your head and say, "Too bad. Rotten luck." Know this:

- THERE IS NO SUCH THING AS LUCK
- YOUR LIFE IS A RESULT OF YOUR HABITUAL THOUGHTS

When you step into a room, perceptive people immediately pick up on your mood, prospective employers sense whether you have adequate confidence in yourself to do the job, and your mate senses whether

You Are A Magnet

you think you are worthy of love. People, employer, and mate all respond to what you expect for yourself.

- *YOUR THOUGHTS PROJECT AND RADIATE ALL THE TIME*

In just the same way, the world — situations, events, natural occurrences — respond to your EXPECTATIONS. The person who thinks he's lucky always seems to be in the right place at the right time. You might ask, "Did he feel lucky because he already had many fortunate things happen to him, or was he thinking optimistically and THEN good things happened to him?"

Thoughts begin everything. We "pray" every minute of our lives. We ask for whatever we think about. We attract it to us. Every single intense thought is answered.

When you set up a certain pattern of thought, everything contrary to that thought is automatically repelled. Everything agreeing with it is automatically attracted to you.

- *YOU ALWAYS MAKE YOURSELF RIGHT*

DAY **13**

For example, if you've had frequent and habitual thoughts about lack of money, you'll attract exactly that condition to you. Even if there's prosperity all around you, it can't possibly come to you or stay with you long until you condition your mind to accept the idea that you will have prosperity. The same is true of weight loss or gain, love, health and every condition in your life.

Fortunate is the person born to wealth, not because he has money, but because that person often develops a prosperity consciousness and expects abundance. His thought patterns attract money, seemingly without much effort. The adage, "You've got to have money to make money," is not true! Money alone does not make money; the expectation of prosperity draws money and success.

- *BELIEFS FORM EXPECTATIONS*
- *WHAT YOU EXPECT IS WHAT YOU GET*

Don't say: "I never get paid what I'm worth," "I'm never going to make it," "Something always goes wrong for me." Your words are magnets. You will prove yourself right! But will that make you happy?

Avoid worrying as well. Why was one person's house robbed, and not their next door neighbor's house? Very little is accidental. When you fear something, you

You Are A Magnet

concentrate energy on that, even if you don't want it. You magnetize even what you fear. Some thoughts have become so habitual, you may not even realize that you're thinking them.

- THINK, SPEAK, EXPECT THE BEST
- EVEN ONE THOUGHT IS A STEP IN THE RIGHT DIRECTION

TODAY'S EXERCISE:

Examine the past events of your life. Write down the major positive events and major negative events that happened to you. Look deep into yourself to see what beliefs you hold or held that attracted those events to you.

TODAY'S THOUGHT:

You are responsible for everything that happens to you. Change your thoughts, and you change your life!

TODAY'S WORDS:

"I am a magnet for everything good!"

DAY **14**

GOOD MORNING! Think about this: you are responsible for everything you experience, at every moment of your day.

Your thoughts, words and beliefs actually create what happens to you. They draw experiences, things and people into your life. Are you resisting this idea? That's not surprising, since for most people, it means looking at life in a totally new way.

We are living this lifetime to become better. That doesn't mean we should act pious or judgmental. It means we're meant to constantly reach for the highest and best in ourselves, to reach for thoughts that are life-enriching: love, understanding, patience, kindness, growth, happiness, abundance.

The world has all these gifts to offer. Life can be a pleasant journey, rewarding and exciting, if you can learn to look at everything and everyone as a means of learning.

In order to do that, you must draw back a little from what's happening to you and look at yourself objectively. Start to ask yourself this question about everything that happens to you:

- *WHAT AM I SUPPOSED TO LEARN FROM THIS SITUATION OR PERSON?*

Every Moment: A Lesson

If you get stuck in dead-end responses, such as anger, blame, jealousy or depression, you not only won't learn anything from the situation, but you'll meet problems with similiar issues in your life over and over until you learn and overcome the lessons!

Until you are able to look at your life with an attitude of objectivity and willingness to learn, you'll just be caught up in the mire, always on the defensive, always reacting instead of acting. But if you can learn to take responsibility for everything that happens in your life, you will start to be in control of it and see that you've always been in control of it.

The following examples will make this clearer:

*EXAMPLE ONE: You may find it difficult to make sufficient money, or you become sick frequently, or accidents and bad luck seem to happen to you often.

TO DO: Take a hard look at what you've been doing. Have you been thinking and talking negatively about these situations? Have you actually asked for and attracted these things, and more of them?

THE LESSON: Vow to think and speak only what you want for yourself. Let negativity flow right out of you when it arises. Be gentle with yourself. You will learn. Practice makes easy.

DAY

14

*EXAMPLE TWO: You didn't get the raise, the relationship, or the job you so desperately wanted.

TO DO: Let's say that in these cases, you did speak and think positively. So what happened? Instead of getting upset, look deep into yourself. Perhaps you have hidden negative beliefs. Maybe you really believe that you're unworthy or powerless. Maybe you believe in scarcity, or that life has to be a struggle. Maybe you fear failure or power.

THE LESSON: Whatever it is, you must have the courage to look at it so you can get rid of it. It's holding you back! Soon, we'll look at ways to help you do this.

*EXAMPLE THREE: You get angry, jealous, or upset.

TO DO: Whenever you find yourself feeling negative reactions, stop. Ask yourself what's really bothering you. Do you get upset when your power, control or security seems threatened? Are your reactions in these situations almost automatic?

THE LESSON: You can't be happy when you're in automatic, reacting like a knee-jerk to situations or people that only seem to threaten your power and security. Learn to hold lightly. You can only own yourself and control yourself, not anyone else.

Every Moment: A Lesson

TODAY'S EXERCISE:

Start to look at every upset and every event that hasn't gone right for you, and ask yourself what you need to learn and see about yourself. If this is difficult, pretend you are a friend who has just come to you for advice. What would you tell that friend?

TODAY'S THOUGHT:

All events reflect your thoughts and fears.

TODAY'S WORDS:

"I'm now getting free from harmful patterns."

DAY 15

GOOD MORNING! Do you know that all the abundance and prosperity you need and want are within your grasp?

Prosperity means peace, health, happiness and plenty in your life. It also means financial abundance: the focus of today's message.

All prosperity begins in the mind. You must first have a prosperous mind-set in order to bring wealth to you. Remember:

- *THOUGHT IS CREATIVE*
- *THOUGHTS ARE POWERFUL ENERGY THAT PROPEL IDEAS INTO REALITY*

Do you have trouble earning money, keeping money, or having enough money to go beyond basic expenses? Know this:

- *THE UNIVERSE IS TOTALLY ABUNDANT; IT'S OUR THINKING THAT'S LIMITED*

Everything you need and want is yours, provided that:

- *YOU BELIEVE IT*
- *YOU TRULY DESIRE IT*
- *YOU ARE WILLING TO ACCEPT IT*

Unlimited Abundance For All

The earth is infinitely good, infinitely rich, infinitely beautiful. You must open up your mind to that truth! The only lack that exists is a lack of understanding on our part.

Why does poverty exist? Because entire groups of people think, talk and expect poverty. They don't know any other way. But you do. Let's stop creating that reality. Every time we make a statement about scarcity in our lives or in the world, we reinforce poverty conditions for ourselves and others. Believe in unlimited abundance for everyone, and you actually help others.

We are meant to have abundance. Poverty is no virtue. It keeps us in slavery, as we focus on providing food and shelter, rather than developing the talents and abilities that are meant to bring joy. The worst thing you can do for the poor is to be one of them. Become prosperous so you can help the entire world to become more prosperous.

Life is meant to be joyful. The more joy you personally experience and the more joyful thoughts you think, the more the entire world becomes that way. Thoughts travel out into the world, affecting everything and everyone around you. By having prosperity, you do not limit anyone else, you actually open up the prosperity possibility for others.

DAY **15**

- *ACCEPT AND BELIEVE IN PROSPERITY FOR YOURSELF*

Look at your habitual thoughts and see whether you're holding yourself back from your good. Can you imagine the world as a wonderful place where everyone can prosper? Try to see abundance for everyone, and everyone benefiting from your abundance. We are all basically loving, and do not want to deprive others with our good fortune. Having what we want in life contributes to the general state of the world's happiness.

Use your imagination to see yourself wealthy, successful, satisfied and fulfilled. Re-read DAY SIX to make sure you understand how to "visualize" your future.

TODAY'S EXERCISE:

Create more prosperity in your life in the following ways:

1. *Give thanks for all the good in your life now.*
2. *Set a financial or material goal that's big enough.*
3. *Visualize having your goal for five minutes each day. See it, feel it, even act as if it's already a reality.*

Unlimited Abundance For All

4. Create an affirmation (as shown in DAY SEVEN) and say or write it, with strong conviction and emotion at least twenty times each day. (i.e., "I now am earning $3,000 each month." "I now have a well-paying job I love." "I am now sailing on my own boat.")

5. Believe that what you want is already on its way to you. Give thanks for it.

6. Release the thought. Don't keep checking to see if it's happening. That sends out feelings of doubt.

7. Do one action each day that shows your trust in your affirmation, even if it's small. (For example: prosperity: Pay 2 cents more for a better product.)

8. Continue this exercise for at least 30 days, even if your desire appears before that time.

TODAY'S THOUGHT:
This is a rich universe, with plenty for all.

TODAY'S WORDS:
"Financial success is coming to me easily."

DAY

GOOD MORNING! You can have everything you need and want, but only if you are ready and willing to receive it!

- *MONEY IS ENERGY AND YOU CONTROL ITS FLOW*

Money is like love: what you have depends on how willing you are to receive it. You may laugh at this and say that you're definitely ready to receive a lot of money, but obviously, something you are doing is standing in your way, if you don't have financial prosperity now.

TODAY'S EXERCISE:

Apply the following to your life.

1. Expect the very best for yourself.

Many of us find it difficult to receive good things in life: money, love, compliments, and so on. Don't blame others for your lack; you'll have only as much as you feel comfortable having.

In order for visualization and affirmations for financial prosperity to work for you, you must be willing to accept what you ask for.

Joyous Receiving

If you can't imagine yourself having a satisfying life in every way, without having to give up anything, take a good look at your self-image. Do you have hidden negative beliefs that you don't deserve the best or that you aren't worthy?

DAY TWENTY FIVE will tell you how to clear this negativity out of your life. But for now: identify your negative belief. You'll recognize it by the pain it causes you to reflect on it. Then: make a strong affirmation to help you counteract it. Examples:

"I deserve to be happy and to have the very best in life."

"I'm a wonderful person just the way I am."

"I'm now willing to be happy and successful."

It's important to say your affirmations frequently and regularly. After all, you're counteracting years of brainwashing yourself negatively. You must clear out your negative beliefs about yourself first, before prosperity affirmations will work well.

DAY **16**

2. *To receive more, start to give more, cheerfully.*

Think of money and wealth as energy, and you'll see that it must move. Money comes to you from others; it flows through you to others. That's how it should be! We receive, we give. Hoarding money is like damming up the circulation. It eventually results in stopping the flow to you.

Whatever you have, there's always something you can give, whether it's time, love, understanding, or something material. Giving and spending with love is very important. When we give in the right spirit, we soon receive many times what we have given.

3. *Create a space for receiving.*

Get rid of what you don't want in order to make room for what you do want. An empty space (a vacuum) draws objects into it; a full space repels new things.

Look in every corner of your life. Clean out whatever you've outgrown, worn out, or don't use. Clean out your closets, dressers, desk, attic and garage. Give items away with love,and with a spirit of totally releasing them, never wanting them back. Don't hold any strings. There's magic in releasing! Letting go allows prosperity to flow in.
Get rid of old ideas, limiting thoughts that are no longer useful. Open your mind to new, nourishing thoughts and they will flow in easily.

Joyous Receiving

4. Forgive everyone and everything in your life.
Forgiveness is another kind of releasing. You release
yourself as well as others. Some people try everything
suggested to bring prosperity, but it remains elusive.
Forgiveness can be the unlocking key. (See tomorrow's
message.)

TODAY'S THOUGHT:
You receive as much as you're willing to have.

TODAY'S WORDS;
"I accept and deserve the best, which is flowing to me
now that I have become an open channel."

DAY 17

GOOD MORNING! Do you use any energy to hold on to past grudges, resentments, and angers?

• UNFORGIVENESS KEEPS GOOD FROM YOU

Just as a blood clot can slow the circulation in your veins and even cause death, old negativity (especially anger and hatred) blocks good things from flowing into your life, can cause ill health, and can prevent certain problems in your life from clearing up.

Forgive sounds dramatic, but the word simply means to "give for" — in other words, to let go in order to make room for something better. When you forgive, you let go of old ideas, feelings, and conditions.

In order to have new, wonderful things flow into your life, you can't be filled up with unresolved issues. Forgiveness brings resolution, and is sometimes the only thing that can be done about a given situation.

Do you have problems in your life that refuse to go away? Are you fighting illness, money problems, things breaking down constantly? Resolution of these problems may not be happening because you're holding on so tightly to all your negative cargo.

Freedom And Forgiveness

Picture anger, hatred, and resentment as black sludge filling up your veins, invading every corner of your body. Many doctors today are linking cancer to the habit of unforgiveness, and that's not surprising. Your mind, body and emotions are closely linked. Every time you have a lingering negative thought, it hurts your body.

Clear out the black sludge! It's weighing you down, gumming you up! Forgive your parents, your spouse, your children, your friends, your enemies. Let the anger come flowing out of you. Think of yourself like a newborn held upside down by your feet. Feel all the black stuff come pouring out of you. Then feel light flowing easily through you.

- REMEMBER TO FORGIVE YOURSELF

The truth is this: Anger, hatred and resentment can mortally wound you. Those feelings work like acid inside you.

When you forgive, finally giving up being angry, when you truly experience letting go of that heavy weight, you may cry or laugh with relief. You won't know how heavy the burden has been until you let go of it. Then you'll be amazed that you carried it for so long. Problems will start to clear up in all parts of your life. You'll feel light and

DAY **17**

free, like a breath of fresh air and sunlight has swept through you.

TÓDAY'S EXERCISE:

Think of a person or situation that brings up negative feelings. Decide that you're ready to get rid of that blockage to your happiness and health. You don't necessarily have to forgive people face to face; doing it in your mind is sometimes all that's necessary.

Here's a miracle-making forgiveness technique: Every day, mentally forgive everyone toward whom you feel negative in any way. Then, if you're holding anger or resentment, if you've criticized or gossiped about anyone, if you're involved in a legal matter with anyone, mentally ask their forgiveness. Yes. Ask their forgiveness of you! Subconsciously, they will respond.

Say:

I fully and freely forgive you. I loose you and let you go. I do not wish to hurt you. I am free and you are free and all is well again between us. I feel love toward you and I glory in your success, prosperity and complete good.

Freedom And Forgiveness

Then, if you have accused yourself of failure or mistakes, forgive yourself.

Say:

I am forgiven and released and all is well.

Repeat both of the above affirmations until you feel release. If necessary, think of the same person day after day, until you feel that you have completely forgiven him or her.

TODAY'S THOUGHT:

Let lightness flow easily through you.

TODAY'S WORDS:

"I free myself by forgiving everyone."

GOOD MORNING! Feeling the glow of love inside you is the single most powerful Super-Charger there is!

Love unifies, harmonizes and balances. Love embodies thoughts of health, prosperity, and happiness. It reminds you that you can do more, be more, experience more of life. Love enriches every part of your life. That's why your waking thoughts of those you love really get you energized.

If you feel unloved and rejected at times, feeling a lack of friends, lover, or family, change your thoughts!

- *START LOVING AND ACCEPTING YOURSELF; THEN GO OUT AND LOVE AND APPRECIATE SOMEONE ELSE*

The more love we give to others, the more love we have. Expand your circle of love to include more and more people. Your joy will double and re-double.

Perhaps you already have a lot of love in your life, but you don't feel as good as you think you should. Because love is such a life-giving, exhilarating, good emotion, something interesting happens when you love a lot, or are loved greatly by someone.

Love Heals

Picture this: you are a clear, tall glass. The negatives in your life — fear, anger, mistrust, negative beliefs — are hard, cold ice cubes at the bottom of the glass. Love is flowing water being poured into you. As love fills up your glass, the ice cubes are forced to the top. You start to feel uncomfortable, upset or angry.

- *LOVE BRINGS UP ANYTHING UNLIKE ITSELF*

This is one of the many reasons why love is such a healthy experience. Even when we think we've got everything ironed out in ourselves, lots of love forces out those last particles of negativity.

- *LOVE IS THE BEST TEACHER*

Don't get scared and run away from your negative feelings. Take a look at your anger, fear, pain, or sadness, and realize that your partner didn't cause it. Your partner may have only activated some past, unresolved negative feelings that needed to be resolved now. Be thankful that he or she helped bring them up.

- *LOVE ALWAYS HEALS, IF YOU LET IT*

DAY **18**

Clear out the negatives and pain lurking in the dark corners of yourself. You may have covered them over for years. Melt those ice cubes!

Let yourself follow those feelings back to their source, and do whatever is necessary to release them! Forgive, accept or create an affirmation. Or do all three. Release yourself!

In that way, you become whole. You learn about yourself and become a better partner.

Being a good partner also means letting love flow. Possessiveness and jealousy are not expressions of love, but expressions of insecurity. You cannot demand love, you can only attract it and receive it. You do this by being a loving, accepting person.

- *ALWAYS TREAT LOVE AS THE MOST PRIZED GIFT*

Heavy expectations drag down a relationship. Love can't flow freely when it's directed. It can cause the stream of love to dam up when a partner sees that his gift, once freely offered, is now being demanded.

- *YOU CANNOT TRULY LOVE WHAT YOU NEED*

Love Heals

Become whole in yourself. Then bring your completed
self to a relationship. You can also do this while you're
involved with someone. Talk about it together so that
you're both aware of the changes.

TODAY'S EXERCISE:
Take stock of your relationships, and write down how
they can assist your growth, if you let them.

TODAY'S THOUGHT:
Open yourself to as much love as you can embrace.

TODAY'S WORDS:
"Giving and accepting love makes me strong."

DAY

GOOD MORNING! Can you remember the last time you felt jealousy? Can you remember the sting, the emptiness, the pain you caused yourself?

Jealousy, corrosive as acid, is probably the most successful killer of relationships. Jealousy is not attractive; it is not a compliment; it does nothing but drive the lover or friend away.

Why does this happen? How do you get it out of your life?

SOURCES OF JEALOUSY:

1. NEED: A belief that, without your lover, your life will be meaningless, you will collapse, and you will never find another lover. This kind of person tries to dump responsibility for creating happiness in his own life at his lover's feet.

2. FEAR: Some people fear that they're easily replaceable. This arises from a lack of sufficient love and respect for one's self.

3. DESIRE FOR CONTROL: If you're hooked on power and manipulation, jealousy is a desire to control a lover's activities. Most likely, this desire has nothing to do with love or caring.

Handling Jealousy

4. *CREATING A LOSING SITUATION: Some people unconsciously want to prove their unworthiness by setting up a jealous situation, thereby causing themselves pain.*

FIRST AID:

1. *BECOME WHOLE IN YOURSELF.*

When you know that you're strong and can take care of yourself, you ARE who you're looking for! You have more to bring to a relationship because there's more of you. By appreciating yourself and being all you need, you learn to accept unconditionally the person you love.

2. *LOVE YOURSELF.*

The more self-esteem and confidence you have, the less likely you are to feel jealous. You can believe you'll find a wonderful new partner if this one goes away. The more you love yourself, the easier it is to love another without conditions.

3. *WE NEVER OWN ANYONE; WE ONLY BORROW THEM FOR A WHILE.*

You cannot control another's love. Period. If you push yourself on someone, it will backfire. You can only attract someone to your side with care and love.

DAY

---

4. LOOK FOR YOUR RESPONSIBILITY IN A BAD SITUATION:

Ask yourself: Did I create this situation to prove that:

- *I'm unworthy?*
- *I'm a failure?*
- *I can never get (or keep) what I want?*
- *Men/women aren't to be trusted?*
- *I always get hurt in love?*
- *I now have an excuse to get rid of my partner?*

• *YOU DON'T HAVE TO REPEAT THIS KIND OF PAIN*

You always set it up (mostly unconsciously) so you learn lessons that are important for you. You can't blame others for your jealousy. You created the situation! Look deeper and you'll uncover your self-defeating patterns. This takes some courage, but when you can see what you do to yourself, you've learned 80% of the lesson. Now you need to act on that awareness.

Handling Jealousy

TODAY'S EXERCISE:

Whenever you find yourself drowning in negative, separating emotions, try first to express love to the person from whom you feel separated. If you're too far gone, take a few deep breaths and really get in touch with what you're feeling. Listen to yourself or pound on a pillow. Then ask yourself: what am I telling myself that's causing these emotions? What's the worst that could happen?

Ask yourself what you need right now. Has this need created these feelings before? Are you willing to let go of that need? Have you had enough suffering?

When you are ready to give up the pain, visualize yourself as you would like to be: strong, free, loving. Start today to break out of your robot-like pattern. Only you can free yourself.

TODAY'S THOUGHT:

Freedom is in choosing to give up pain.

TODAYS' WORDS:

"I am now ready to give up control. I no longer hurt myself. I am strong and wonderful and free."

DAY 20

GOOD MORNING! Think for a moment about this:

• EVERY PERSON IN YOUR LIFE IS YOUR TEACHER

What do they teach you, you ask? They teach you about yourself. So give thanks for every person in your life, even if you wish they weren't there. Here's why:

• YOU TEND TO ATTRACT WHAT YOU ARE

If you're not happy with the kind of friends or lovers you have in your life, remember that what you radiate you will attract. Other people are our mirrors. What you don't like about another may very well be what you don't like about yourself.

• NO OTHER PERSON CAN CONTROL YOU

Give up being afraid of other people. No one has control over you unless you give it to him. If you dislike being around other people because you fear manipulation, ask yourself what you're supposed to learn from the situation. Do you need to learn to crave less approval or to trust your intuition more?

Learn From Everyone

- *THE GREATEST FRICTION MAY YIELD THE LARGEST LESSON*

Certain people activate our irritation. Whenever you feel stongly negative around someone, study your reactions. Do you feel that your security or power is threatened? Can you let go of that security and power, or are you addicted to it?

Dependency and strong needs for security and power can only result in unhappiness. We need to learn to have a "light hand" with everything. Otherwise, we could spend our lives in irritation. Be thankful for these situations: they've given you the opportunity to see where you need to grow.

- *HELP OTHERS WITHOUT BUYING INTO THEIR PROBLEMS*

You can be supportive of others in a loving, compassionate way, but don't try to remove obstacles for them. Every obstacle and problem has been put in each of our lives so we can learn. The problems of others are offering them messages they need for their growth, just as your problems are offering you messages for your growth. You can be compassionate without getting caught up in their dramas.

DAY **20**

• *HELP OTHERS ONLY WHEN YOU CAN EMOTIONALLY
AFFORD TO GIVE*

*When you resent helping someone, or if you do it out of
guilt, you create even more of a problem. The other
person feels intuitively that he is a burden. You cannot
hide your feelings. Remain happy and loving, and at the
same time, learn from your friend's suffering. However,
you are not obligated to indulge their negativity. Gently
guide them to positive talk, or leave.*

• *TREAT EACH OTHER WITH KINDNESS*

*We are all on a path of learning. From time to time,
everyone is afraid and vulnerable. Give each person you
meet the benefit of the doubt, no matter how aloof or
tough he may seem.*

• *IF POSSIBLE, AVOID SPEAKING OR ACTING WHEN
UPSET*

Learn From Everyone

Bad feelings are contagious. When you interact with anger, resentment or fear, other people will mirror your feelings almost immediately. When upset, your wisdom and love are inhibited, and what you say and do will probably be a selection of your power or security addictions. The result: no one will be perceptive or understanding, and the goal (resolution) will be totally forgotten. The encounter won't be satisfying to anyone, including you.

TODAY'S EXERCISE:

Look at everyone you are around today with new eyes. Try to see the lesson each person is showing you about yourself. Repeat TODAY'S WORDS aloud twenty times.

TODAY'S THOUGHT:

Treat everyone as a precious, temporary gift.

TODAY'S WORDS:

"Everyone around me helps me to grow."

SECTION III: You and the Future - An In-Depth Look

DAY 21

GOOD MORNING! Happiness begins with having loving
regard for yourself. If you can love yourself in the
forgiving, accepting way that you love your family and
friends, you'll trust your own inner directions.

What is inner direction? You might call it intuition, gut
feel, a sudden flash of knowing, or even just a strong
compulsion to use certain abilities.

- *YOUR INNER MESSAGES SHOULD NEVER BE
  IGNORED*

They tell you what's right for you. They are the guidelines
for action in your life, and very often, far superior to
analysis and logic.

Studies show that chief executives in large corporations,
after examining statistics and other information, ultimately
rely on their gut feel. Yet many people ignore these
messages.

From time to time, you're faced with difficult decisions:
whether to accept a job, get married, move to a new
location, and dozens of other daily decisions. If you listen
to yourself, the answer comes swiftly. But if you don't
have a loving regard for yourself, you may not trust
yourself enough to listen to, and act upon, the messages
that your inner self is sending to you.

Listen To Yourself

What does it mean to have a loving regard for yourself? It means you acknowledge that:

- *YOUR LIFE, YOUR NEEDS AND YOUR DESIRES ARE IMPORTANT*

You look kindly upon your imperfections, knowing that you will make every effort to learn and understand. You can't love yourself and hate your emotions at the same time. Don't get upset with yourself when you find that you're dwelling on negative issues in your life. Instead, ask yourself gently why you are doing so. In quietness, and with a kind attitude toward yourself, your intuition will give you the answer.

Your inner direction is the key to choosing what's best for you. But you'll be confused if you're caught up in being disgusted with yourself, feeling unworthy, and comparing yourself to others. In that weakened position, you're bound to be influenced by the expectations and dogmas of others, to such an extent that you might succumb to seeking their approval rather than your own. You'll be vulnerable to manipulation.

What is the result of ignoring our intuitions? Surely you've experienced many already: uncomfortable, stressful

DAY **21**

situations; repression of feelings; headaches, ulcers, and other physical signs that you're not acting in accordance with what's right for you. And of course, you've wasted time. When you start down the wrong road, sooner or later you've got to turn around and retrace your your steps.

TODAY'S EXERCISE:

Begin to be aware of all the signals you get from yourself. That quiet, small voice may come only as a hunch, a flash of certainty. Or the message may come to you through physical upset. However, emotional explosion is not a message from your intuition; it's a result of built-up frustration over uncomfortable decisions that you've already made. Get calm before taking action.

Today, write down past and present instances where you have trusted yourself and acted on your intuition, and those times when you haven't. Write also the factors you believe prevented you from following your intuition.

But remember: other people don't cause us to do anything. They aren't the reason we do anything. Lack of self-esteem, mistrust of our inner instincts, and a sense of powerlessness are the real culprits.

Listen To Yourself

Start now to say TODAY'S WORDS below at least twenty times a day. Know that you are powerful, that it is right to trust yourself, that your intuitions are telling you something very important. Refuse to accept doubt and fear.

Every time you get tense and irritable, stop for a few moments. Get in touch with your inner wisdom and find out what you need and want at this moment. You don't have to get it at this moment, but you'll relax just by acknowledging it.

TODAY'S THOUGHT:

Intuition is not merely a hunch, but is an irresistable light which must be followed.

TODAY'S WORDS:

"I trust myself and believe in my innate wisdom."

DAY **22**

GOOD MORNING! *Do you want to be lean, energetic, optimistic, and finish your day's list without getting tired? Do you want radiant skin, sparkling eyes and a spring in your step? Do you want better control over your moods so you won't suddenly be overtaken by feeling low? Do you want to get so healthy that you'll never have another cold? How?*

The answer is simple. It's not even a secret.

Eating for success can be learned much more easily than dressing for it. Super energy eating provides your body with the right fuel so that it looks, feels and performs at its best.

- *WHAT YOU PUT IN YOUR BODY AFFECTS EVERYTHING ABOUT YOU*

Not only your body, but your brain is also affected by the food you eat. Eating super energy food and excluding drag-down food will not only give you a high energy body and a wonderful appearance, it will help you reason and think more clearly and have a better memory. You'll actually feel more intelligent, work more efficiently and accomplish much more in less time.

Super Energy Food

How do I sign up, you ask? First, understand this:

- *LIVE FOOD PRODUCES A VIBRANTLY ALIVE BODY*
- *DRAG-DOWN FOOD PRODUCES A TIRED BODY*

TODAY'S EXERCISE:
From today to the end of these 30 days, you will start to eat more super energy food. Because food makes such a remarkable difference in the way you feel, this book wouldn't be complete without a prescription for physical health and well-being.

SUPER ENERGY FOOD HEALTH PRESCRIPTION:
1. Cut out all, or almost all, drag-down and dead foods:

   - Beef, pork, chicken, even fish are animal carcasses. At the very minimum, cut out red meat. It takes hours to digest this heavy protein. You can get protein from vegetables, grains, even certain fruits. The human system was not designed to handle meat digestion.

   - Dairy products. Adult digestive systems are not equipped to digest these foods. Dairy products produce abdominal gas, bad skin, and prevent the absorption of nutrients.

DAY

- Salt, sugar, refined foods, chemically preserved foods, white bread, white rice. Boxed, canned, even frozen foods are dead. The FDA won't allow food (other than produce) to be sold in a grocery store unless it's dead.

2. Drink at least ten 8 oz. glasses of water each day, preferably distilled or bottled.

   - Add a touch of lemon or lime juice. Water flushes your system of impurities, clears your skin, and slims you. It's like priming a pump. If you don't do it, chemical "trash" collects in your body, in your liver, your intestines, your skin tissues. Don't drink with your meals; stop drinking a half-hour before meals and start again two hours after meals to avoid interfering with digestion.

3. Eat only live foods, primarily vegetables and fruits.

   - For lunch and dinner, eat loads of vegetables, as many raw as possible. Try sprouts: they're one of the best foods you can eat. Get them from almost any grocery store, or grow them yourself. The more you eat, the better. They'll slim your body fast. If cooking, avoid oils and fats and over-cooking.

Super Energy Food

- *Eat fruits as a meal. Do not eat them with vegetables. Try an entire breakfast of fruits (no more than four kinds.)*

4. *In general: eat simply.*

   - *Don't eat when upset or overly tired or within 3-4 hours of going to bed. Eat only when hungry. Stop before you're full. Study a a food-combining chart or book.*

- *LIVE FOODS — A SLIMMER, SMARTER, STRONGER AND MORE SUCCESSFUL YOU*

TODAY'S THOUGHT:
Give your body the best!

TODAY'S WORDS:
"I put only the best fuel into my body."

DAY 23

GOOD MORNING! Did you know that you can survive weeks without food, three days without water, but only three minutes without air? Air is our most vital fuel. Most of us don't get enough of it.

The lungs act as a bellows, increasing the pressure in our bodies, forcing the blood to circulate faster, and as a result, the heart gets exercise. All tissue needs exercise to remain strong and elastic. And when more blood is circulating in your brain, you think more clearly and quickly.

When you intake sufficient oxygen, interior and exterior wounds heal more quickly, blood is purified, and you feel energetic. When you become tense, you probably breathe shallowly, and eventually feel exhausted. The solution is to get enough oxygen to your system by a series of slow, deep breaths.

However, even if you breathe properly, if you smoke, you probably aren't getting enough oxygen. Doctors will tell you that even one cigarette damages the tiny oxygen-absorbing fibers in your lungs (cilia).

Oxygen wakes up your system. It re-activates you when you're tired. Slow, deep breathing is great when you're confined to a desk or must remain stationary, but exercise is even better.

Jumping Jacks And Air Fuel

- *EXERCISE WAKES YOU UP, BOTH MENTALLY AND PHYSICALLY*

Feel more alive! Get exercise every single day. Every day, you'll feel increasingly more energy.

- *EXERCISE IS MEDICINE, FOR MIND, BODY AND SOUL*

Mind and body are connected. Just as your thoughts can dramatically affect the state of your body, the vitality of your body and its chemical balance can affect your thoughts. Many recent studies show that daily exercise can alleviate all types of mental problems, including depression.

- *EXERCISE IS EXHILARATING*

Here are just a few of the benefits of daily exercise:

1. *More energy.*
2. *Less sleep requirements.*
3. *More restful sleep.*
4. *Physical tension gets drained away.*
5. *Hormones preventing depression are produced.*

DAY **23**

6. Other hormones give you an exercise "high."

7. Metabolism rate increases for up to 24 hours.

8. Appetite is dulled.

9. A slimmer, sleeker body after just two weeks.

10 A stronger, more flexible body.

11. Radiant attractiveness following a work-out.

12. More control of yourself and your world.

13. Recommended by therapists for mental health.

14. Skin condition can dramatically improve.

Do you drag home from work at the end of the day feeling exhausted? Stress and anxiety can rob you of energy. Instead of dragging through the evening, immediately change into comfortable clothes and try a few jumping jacks, or just jump up and down.

You may feel tired at first, but keep going for at least three minutes. Don't stop moving until the end of that time! After about three minutes, your body will start to release tension and you'll feel more energetic. Keep going!

However, if you don't start to perk up, then you probably should take a short nap. After that, you'll be twice as productive in the evening.

Jumping Jacks And Air Fuel

Listen to your body. Don't fill yourself up with caffeine at night; take a siesta. Even 15 minutes of quiet rest can rejuvenate you.

TODAY'S EXERCISE:

From now until the end of these 30 days, get 15 to 60 minutes of exercise each day. Walking, running, aerobics, whatever feels good. Work hard one day, cut back the next. ANY amount of aerobic exercise (running, jumping rope, aerobic dancing, bicycle riding, etc.) gets your mind and body working much better! Just do something. You'll feel great.

TODAY'S THOUGHT:

Exercise makes joy!

TODAY'S WORDS:

"I look and feel better every day."

DAY 24

GOOD MORNING! High energy, health, joyousness in our physical selves: that's our birthright! So why do many people spend their lives combatting illness? Why do you get sick at all?

You've seen how your words and thoughts create what you experience in your life. You know now that you must take responsibility for having created everything that happens to you. So, too, you create illness in your life.

Listen to the words around you: "I always get sick in the winter." "I get everything that's going around."

Remember: We create it. We always get to be right. If you say that's how it will be for you, then that's how you'll get it.

Health is an excellent example of the connection between thoughts and their results. If you focus on illness or fear of becoming sick, your mental image will become reality.

- *SEE YOURSELF PERFECTLY HEALTHY, RADIANT AND STRONG*
- *FOCUS ON HEALTH*
- *FORGET ABOUT ILLNESS*

Radiant Health

Try it! It works. What is there to lose? Sympathy? The ritual of complaining? There's so much to gain! Let go of illness; let go of anything preventing you from being all you can be.

Some negative beliefs can be changed overnight. In that case, you'll see an immediate change in your health for the better. But other beliefs are more deeply ingrained, and you'll have to work on yourself to change. You don't have to get sick.

However, when you're already sick, it's sometimes difficult to feel that your life is in your control. During illness, take a five minute break three times daily to concentrate on how you'll feel when you're gloriously healthy again. Focus your thoughts on strength, energy and joy. Put your energy there, and forget completely about your condition. You'll soon feel the positive power of your thoughts. You'll be on your feet much faster.

What goes on in your mind — your thoughts and words expressing strength and well-being — are actually more important than what you eat or what you do. But, exercise and the right kind of food will give you the enthusiasm to focus on health-giving thoughts! When you begin to feel good, it's easier to say:

"Hey, I feel great! I'm full of energy!"

DAY 24

"I'm so strong, I'm always going to feel healthy!"

- *YOUR THOUGHTS ARE THE POWER-BOOSTER FOR YOUR BODY'S HEALTH*

Don't talk about your aches and pains to other people, because you then focus on the discomfort, and actually make it worse. Focus on whatever positive things you can find.

Moreover, when other people start telling you about their illnesses, encourage them to talk about how they intend to get healthy, or encourage them to say that they'll get better soon. If they can't do either, encourage them to stop talking about it altogether. Don't be a party to prolonging their illness.

This doesn't make you an unsympathetic person. It makes you and them aware that, for the most part, we choose to be sick, or to stay sick, or to become more sick.

- *CHOOSE HEALTH*
- *THINK HEALTH*

The only limits on our health, energy and vitality come from your own mind: negative beliefs, barriers, and resistance to the goodness of life.

Radiant Health

TODAY'S EXERCISE:

Talk only health, energy and positive things. You may feel tired and sick, but why focus on it? It does nothing but make you (and the person you're talking with) feel worse.

If you find yourself unwilling to give up talking about your aches and pains, ask yourself what you're getting out of holding on to the negative. Does it get you out of doing something? Does it give you a break so you can stay home? If so, start learning other ways of having space and time, so you won't have to get sick to get what you want! It's not worth it!

TODAY'S THOUGHT:

Our natural state is to have radiant health, boundless energy, and vitality throughout our lives.

TODAY'S WORDS:

"I give thanks for ever-increasing health, beauty and vitality."

DAY **25**

GOOD MORNING! Are your beliefs assets or liabilities? Beliefs are your deep assumptions about life. Whether positive or negative, they create your life and act as a filter through which you see everything. Root beliefs are the most fundamental assumptions and expectations we have of how life will treat us.

- *NEGATIVE BELIEFS CAN KEEP YOU STUCK IN FAILURE*
- *THROW THEM OUT OF YOUR LIFE*

Some of these negative beliefs might be ideas you formed very early in life. You may not even realize how much they affect you right now. When negative beliefs are buried deepest, they are the most dangerous. However, when we become consciously aware of our negative beliefs, they cause fewer problems.

Some of these fundamental negative beliefs have been mentioned before, but they bear repeating here:

- *Life is a struggle.*
- *It can never be easy for me.*
- *I'm helpless.*

Clear Out Negative Beliefs

- *- I don't deserve to be happy.*
- *- I'm not worthy of being loved.*
- *- Other people hurt me.*
- *- I have to do without things I need.*
- *- I wasn't meant to have money.*

There are many more. Find out whether you're carrying around some of these negative beliefs. They may be preventing you from having what you want in life.

If strong negative beliefs are running you, you must get rid of them before affirmations and visualization can work effectively for you. For example, prosperity can't come to you if you firmly believe that life will always be a struggle. Affirmations to find the perfect partner won't work if you fundamentally believe that you don't deserve to have the best, or if you believe that lasting harmony isn't possible. There are all kinds of ways to sabotage what you want in life. Perhaps you are now becoming aware of how you may be sabotaging yourself.

Whenever you find an area of your life that's not working well — relationships, job, money — start looking for the negative belief that's damming up the works. You might be surprised that you've been holding on to that negative thought.

DAY **25**

How do you find out what your beliefs are? Here are two ways:

1. *The most direct method is to have a series of talks with yourself. Write down your beliefs in a variety of areas. You'll probably find out that you believe different things at different times. Sometimes contradictions will be easy to spot. These opposing beliefs affect your body and emotions. Examine the conflicts you find.*

2. *The second method starts from the emotions, rather than the intellect. Whenever you feel strong negative emotion, such as, "I'm a failure," start to see that your emotions are probably not statements of fact. You may feel like a failure, while actually being a good student, mother, etc.*

By seeing that there is a difference between what your emotions are saying ("I'm a failure") and what is actually true in reality, you will begin to catch a glimpse of the negative beliefs that have been causing you problems, perhaps for years.

Clear Out Negative Beliefs

As you become more and more honest with yourself, you
will begin to recognize other root negative emotions.
Then you may more completely understand the
statement: "You are responsible for creating your reality."
You may have said: "But I'm not responsible for being
poor!" Now you understand that a belief such as feeling
unworthy could have prevented you from being wealthy
in the past. How do you change this? See below.

TODAY'S EXERCISE:

Take time today to pinpoint one of your root negative
beliefs. Then, use affirmations to start the process of
change. For example, a belief that you are unworthy can
be wiped out by persistently affirming: "I deserve the best
in life." Create an affirmation that specifically attacks your
old programming and say it aloud twenty times, three
times daily. This is very important.

TODAY'S THOUGHT:

Whatever you believe deeply will show up in your life.

TODAY'S WORDS:

"I am now ready to clear up any beliefs that hold me
back from the good I want in life."

DAY 26

GOOD MORNING! Perhaps you've found that, despite all your good intentions, certain thoughts are stuck in negativity. Don't worry. When you find an area of your life that refuses to give way to light and happiness, you just need a special technique to help you take a look at it in a new way so you can release it.

You've learned that your thoughts create what happens to you. You know if you focus on negativity, you'll only get more of it. Because you understand this, you might be a little afraid of your own negative thoughts and feelings. Don't be.

• DON'T SUPPRESS RECURRING NEGATIVE EMOTION

This might sound inconsistent with what you've been reading, but it isn't. On Days One and Two, you learned that casual negative statements and thoughts are damaging to you. You're ridding your life of those negatives.

But today's message is not concerned with momentary negatives that are easy to change; today's message concerns situations you've struggled with for a long time, perhaps years.

Handling Persistent Negativity

These major negative issues in your life are like large black barriers. Whenever you think of them, you start to feel anger, hatred, fear or helplessness. Perhaps you feel tearful. If you have an area in your life like this, read on with special care.

TODAY'S EXERCISE:

Try this whenever negative emotion grabs you:

1. Don't fight the emotion. Don't get involved with it, either. Step back and observe yourself.

Trying to stop strong negative emotion doesn't solve the problem in this case. Follow the feeling so you can get at the root of it. In that way, you can finally release it. This book is not about smiling when you don't feel happy. It's about taking a good look at yourself, examining difficult areas in your life, and clearing them out, so you can be genuinely happy!

2. Look deep inside to find out what you're telling yourself or what negative belief you have that's creating this emotion. Getting a clear view of your own beliefs is the most essential part of this exercise. Your beliefs are the source of your emotions.

Some beliefs are obvious to us; others are hidden. But we always act upon our beliefs and we see the world through them. You attract events and people that reflect your beliefs.

Without examining your beliefs, your negative emotions won't budge. For example, you can't decide to be happy if you carry the belief that you don't have a right to be happy, or if you believe that you aren't worthy of happiness.

As you become aware of your beliefs, you'll see how they automatically bring forth certain emotions. The free flow of your emotions will always bring you back to your beliefs, if you don't stand in the way. This process is for understanding your emotions, not rising above them. Stay in touch with yourself.

3. When you root out and identify your negative beliefs, they're already on their way to being cleaned out of your life. The real troublemakers in your life are beliefs you don't know you have and that continue to get in your way.

Our most fundamental assumptions about life are often most deeply hidden. You may have acquired them at a very young age.

Handling Persistent Negativity

Are some of these negative beliefs hurting you?

- Life is a struggle.

- I'm powerless.

- I'm unworthy.

- I don't trust myself.

- There's not enough. I have to do without.

4. MOST IMPORTANT: Create special "clearing" affirmations to counteract the negative beliefs you've been carrying around. Say them often in quiet moments. See TODAY'S WORDS for examples.

TODAY'S THOUGHT:

What you believe to be true, you create.

TODAY'S WORDS:

"I deserve to be happy, healthy and wealthy."

"Life is fun and pleasurable."

"It's all right for me to be successful."

"I trust myself."

"I always have everything I need."

"I am responsible for creating my life."

"I have control of my life."

DAY **21**

GOOD MORNING! Today you're going to get out your map and compass and find out where you are in your life, and where you want to be!

Do you have goals you've never told anyone because you feared they were impossible dreams? Do you have a goal that you do talk about, but don't seem to get closer to as the years go by? Are you uncertain about what your goals are?

We all have ideas about what we want to do, be or have in life. Those who say they can't define their goals generally have too many "shoulds" weighing them down. Listen to yourself, trust yourself, and you'll find the answers. You need to point in the direction you want.

- *YOU'RE ALWAYS GOING SOMEWHERE; MAKE SURE IT'S WHERE YOU WANT TO GO*

You can't stop the motion of your life. Even if you've put off deciding on a direction or goal, you have drifted somewhere.

Choosing goals takes courage and trust. You stick your neck out a little. Even if you don't tell anyone about your goal, YOU know it's what you want.

Charting Your Course

- *DARE TO GET BEHIND YOUR PLAN 100% AND YOU'LL SUCCEED*

Failure is caused by hedging bets. It's caused by being reluctant to talk and act as if you're already successful.

Do you think an affirmation like the following would be helpful? -- "I think I kind of want to get started as a building contractor, but if I don't, I can always keep working as a carpenter."

Will that thought impact his sub-conscious mind positively? No. Will it take him anywhere? Probably not. Commit to yourself. Commit to your goal. That person should affirm every morning: "I am now a building contractor." He or she should think it, feel it, radiate it!

And what happens next? Everything he needs will begin to appear in his life. Perhaps he'll meet the right people or hear about an opportunity.

TODAY'S EXERCISE:
1. *FIND YOUR GOALS AND DECIDE NOW TO GO AFTER THEM! Intense desire makes things happen!*
2. *WRITE YOUR GOALS DOWN. Writing goals is magical. And writing gives you a plan, rather than a wish or a daydream. Writing steadies a commitment.*

DAY **27**

---

3. READ YOUR GOALS EVERY DAY.

You will reinforce your commitment and inspire action.

4. VISUALIZE REACHING YOUR GOAL.

Experts say the best times are just after awakening, and just before falling asleep. See yourself as you will feel after reaching your goal.

5. MAKE AN AFFIRMATION FOR YOUR GOAL AND AFFIRM YOURSELF.

Affirmations are the fuel for motion. Affirm your goal many times each day. Keep building your confidence. Repeat today's words aloud 10 times, 3 times daily.

6. AVOID THE NEGATIVITY OF OTHERS.

Be strong in your course. Don't absorb the failure mind-sets of other people.

7. KNOW THAT YOU ARE IN CONTROL OF YOUR LIFE.

8. ACT AS IF YOU'VE ALREADY ACHIEVED YOUR GOAL!

9. TAKE ACTION! SEIZE OPPORTUNITIES!

Charting Your Course

All of your abilities, talents and intuition are waiting, like a regiment of soldiers, to be called upon to help you achieve your goals. When you commit to a goal, everything inside and outside of you responds to get you there.

But without a plan, a stated goal, your soldiers dash one way and then another, splitting up and therefore working ineffectively. Would you ever get into a taxi and tell the driver you didn't know where you wanted to go?

- *DECIDE ON A DESTINATION*

Don't spend your life in frustration. Don't reach age sixty or seventy and whine about what you never did. Find out what you truly want, and discard outgrown desires. Change your goal if you discover it isn't the right one. You're in charge!

TODAY'S THOUGHT:
"Whatever you can do, or dream you can do, begin it. Boldness has genius, power, and magic in it." -Goethe

TODAY'S WORDS:
"I have what it takes to do anything I aim for."

DAY 28

GOOD MORNING! Success and self-confidence go hand-in-hand. When you cultivate one, you automatically cultivate the other. The more self-confident you are, the more you'll actually attract your success to you!

• *THOUGHTS OF SUCCESS CREATE SUCCESS*

When you are trying to create success in any area of your life, or to change your beliefs about yourself, look through your past with the concepts from this book in mind. Look for the good times, the successes, the positive aspects.

• *REVIEW AND INTENSIFY MEMORIES OF PAST SUCCESS*

This approach is very different from the current manner in which we have learned to look at our lives. In general, if we have a problem area in our lives, we tend to examine the past, looking for where it went wrong. That method makes it worse!

• *STOP SELF-DEFEATING REVIEWS OF THE PAST*

It cannot be emphasized too strongly that reviewing failures will only create more. Stressing negatives makes you blind to the positives. Stressing positives makes them grow!

Success And Self-Confidence

Change your beliefs about your own past! If you felt deprived as a child, start trying to remember the good times and emphasize them. If you felt a failure, poor, sick, or any lack or limitation in your life, stop focusing on those memories!

What you remember will seem to justify your present beliefs. Therefore, some people believe they are sickly, or unlucky because they constantly review memories of sickness and bad luck. They've spent a lot of time schooling themselves in holding onto negative labels of their lives. Learn how to escape the negative cycles.

Take any area of your life and remember a time, even one, when your label didn't hold true. If sick, remember a time when you were not. If poor, remember a time when you were free of money worries.
- *YOU CAN ACTUALLY RESHAPE YOUR PAST*
- *YOU CAN START TO SEE YOURSELF AS A FREE, NEW PERSON*

When you look for positive signposts from your past, you actually begin to feel better about yourself. Confidence begins to grow.

- *REINFORCE YOUR CONFIDENCE*

DAY **28**

Although confidence radiates from the inner to the outer person, paying attention to your appearance can actually help you to be more confident. Here are some ways you can do that.

TODAY'S EXERCISE:

1. If there's anything you don't like about your body, begin today to change whatever is within your control. Create an affirmation for that particular area. Examples: "I can now lose weight steadily and easily."

2. Wear your best clothes. That's part of prosperity thinking. Make yourself feel good every day! Don't wait for a special occasion. Treat yourself well. Try wearing your best clothes every day for a week and see how it feels.

3. Buy only high quality clothing. You don't have to spend a lot of money on clothes. Own two or three high quality outfits and wear them with more frequency.

• *EXPAND YOUR CONFIDENCE WITH AFFIRMATIONS*

Affirmations are such wonderful things! Use them when you're feeling doubts about yourself and they'll lift you

Success And Self-Confidence

up. Confidence is healthy, productive, and energizing. If you love yourself, you'll give more love to others.

Confidence is not being egotistical and closed to growth and new ideas. It's not refusing to consider suggestions from others. If you have any negative thoughts about having confidence, get rid of them! Confidence is the first, most important building block in your life.

SOME LIFE-ENHANCING AFFIRMATIONS:

- I do the best things for myself.
- I'm so beautiful today!
- I can do anything I decide to do.
- I love my body and keep it healthy.
- Other people find me fascinating and terrific.
- Other people love to have me around.
- Everyone believes in me.

TODAY'S THOUGHT:

Believe in yourself and all things are possible!

TODAY'S WORDS:

"Every day, I have more and more confidence!"

DAY 29

GOOD MORNING! *Every day is a miniature view of your life: lessons that need to be learned, barriers that need work, giving and receiving, forgiving, relationships, and steps taken toward what you want in your life.*

Going to sleep with a clear mind and a heart at peace helps you to sleep better and wake up refreshed. Start tonight to take a few minutes to assess your day. Making a habit of the following steps will help you to stay in touch with yourself:

1. *REVIEW THE DAY:*

   - *Forgive yourself and others for any negative incident.*

   - *If anything went wrong today, see yourself going through it again exactly the way you wish you had.*

   - *Either mentally or in reality, clean up all relationships.*

   - *Release all the incidents of the day and don't allow them to haunt you later.*

Completing Your Day

---

2. CHECK YOUR PROGRESS TOWARD YOUR GOALS:

- Review the efforts today that brought you closer to your goals. Concentrate on your most important goal.
- If you didn't take steps toward your goal today, acknowledge that, but don't focus on it or worry.
- Mentally set up what you want to accomplish tomorrow, and your subconscious mind will quietly go to work on it at night.

3. ASK YOURSELF WHAT LESSONS YOU'VE LEARNED TODAY:

- What lessons do you need to try again?
- This is the time to be objective about all the upsets you had today. What were you supposed to learn?

4. TAKE A READING OF YOUR PHYSICAL SELF:

- Are you eating super-energy, alive foods?
- Are you drinking at least 10 glasses of water?
- Did you do some kind of exercise today?

5. SET UP YOUR DREAMS:

- *Choose an area in your life that you'd like to improve, make a decision about, or get more information on: your goals, career, relationships, house, health . . . anything that's important to you.*

Starting to work with a plan like this might seem cumbersome at first, but you'll be amazed at how quickly this becomes routine, and how fast your mind can work. You can accomplish all of these steps in less than five minutes.

Americans have been told that we need eight hours of sleep. New studies are showing that people who sleep five or six hours, with a nap later, may be more in touch with their intuition and creativity than those who sleep longer.

If you'd like to shorten your sleeping time, do it gradually over a period of a few weeks. Shorten it by no more than fifteen minutes every couple of nights. Soon you'll be sleeping less and feeling better.

Some people find it helpful to take a short nap in the late afternoon or early evening. Sometimes even fifteen minutes can revive you, but in any case, nap for no longer than two hours, or you'll wake feeling groggy.

Completing Your Day

TODAY'S EXERCISE:

Start tonight to follow this plan. You'll be amazed at what a good feeling it will give you.

TODAY'S THOUGHT:

Everything you need to know is inside you.

TODAY'S WORDS:

"In quietness, I find the answer to every problem."

DAY 30

GOOD MORNING! This is the last day of your 30 DAYS TO HAPPINESS program. But it doesn't have to be the last time you pick up this book. You can use it over and over every thirty days until the new concepts have become deeply rooted in you.

Change happens with repetition and time. But change can also happen overnight if you have a strong desire to change, a willingness to accept new ideas, and an ability to visualize clearly how you want to be, think, or act.

There are no rules about how fast or slowly you or your life will change. It's entirely up to you — and what you believe. Remember:

- *YOU ALWAYS MAKE YOURSELF RIGHT; SO, BE RIGHT ABOUT POSITIVE IDEAS*

This book is about possibility; it's about leaping beyond where you've been into the person you've always wanted to be.

This book is also about responsibility: keeping your thoughts, words, and imagination focused on the best you want for yourself.

You can do anything, be anything, have anything — in whatever amount of time you've told yourself it has to take.

Changing Your Life

- *THERE ARE NO LIMITS, EXCEPT THE ONES YOU SET FOR YOURSELF*

Change is not always easy. Habits, even the worst ones, are comfortable because they're familiar. Getting rid of old ways of talking and thinking might make you feel lost at first. That's natural. Many people have become comfortable with terrible, demeaning circumstances.

- *DON'T STAY COMFORTABLE WITH: DEPRESSION, FEAR, ANGER, POVERTY, ILLNESS, LOW ENERGY, STRUGGLE, CONFLICT, BAD RELATIONSHIPS*
- *AFTER THINGS GET BETTER, DON'T GET SCARED*
- *DON'T GET UNCOMFORTABLE WITH HOW GOOD IT IS*

For example, don't make waves in smooth relationships because the only ones you've experienced have been hard work! If you expect the boom to fall, you know now that in some way, you yourself will cause it to fall.

Remember: When you change, getting rid of old negative patterns, you might feel empty, lost, sad, uncertain, or confused. Those feelings will pass. You have simply created a vacuum for good thoughts and patterns to flow

DAY **30**

---

in. Don't fill up the new space with a different negative pattern!

With a little practice and time, you'll get used to the new you. You might slip and go back to the old pattern for a little while.Don't get upset with yourself. Just get back on track. You'll be stronger each time. The new you will bring you so much more happiness, love, money, satisfaction and health, you'll soon give up going back to the old ways.

- *PERSIST WITH YOUR DREAMS; THEY'LL BECOME REAL*

- *FILL YOURSELF WITH LOVE AND ALWAYS EXPECT THE BEST*

TODAY'S EXERCISE:

1. *Review this book often. Some days, you may want to read only one passage; other days, you may want to read more. Repeat this 30 DAYS TO HAPPINESS often. Each time you do, it will be a new experience. The first time through, you've probably analyzed the new concepts, and perhaps even resisted some of them. Each time you do the 30 DAYS TO HAPPINESS again, you'll want to work more with goals, affirmations, and visualization.*

Changing Your Life

2. Underline the sentences in this book that are important to you. These are concepts you're now ready to absorb. As you re-read this book, you'll want to underline more. The new markings will show you your changes and your progress toward a greater understanding.

3. Offer these ideas to others, but only if they are receptive. They have their paths to follow, in their own time.

4. Keep up a strong desire to make your life happier. Intense desire actually attracts good things to you. Your life will improve by leaps and bounds! It's only up to you!

TODAY'S THOUGHT:

You create everything in your life!

TODAY'S WORDS:

"I congratulate myself on completing this 30 DAYS TO HAPPINESS!"

COMPLETION

DAY:	1	2	3	4	5	6	7
DAY'S READING:							
DAY'S EXERCISE:							
DAY'S AFFIRMATIONS:							
SUPER-CHARGER:							

DAY:	20	21	22	23	24	25	26
DAY'S READING:							
DAY'S EXERCISE:							
DAY'S AFFIRMATIONS:							
SUPER-CHARGER:							

CHART:

8	9	10	11	12	13	14	15	16	17	18	19

27	28	29	30

Put a checkmark in each box you complete every day. This method will help you keep track of your progress.

ABOUT THE AUTHOR

Liah Kraft-Kristaine, a peak performance expert, draws upon experience in communications, law, business and the arts. She is an international seminar leader, a celebrated keynote speaker, author of six books, and the host of a PBS television special, The Myths of Happiness.

She holds a Juris Doctorate Degree from Emory University, Bachelor Degrees in Philosophy and Humanities, and has studied for a post-graduate degree in transpersonal psychology. In the past, she has been a practicing attorney, Hollywood scriptwriter, actress, and television program host for Cable News Network.

Ms. Kraft-Kristaine has recorded on cassette the entirety of this book, 30 Days to Happiness.   This four-cassette book-on-tape program is available through LMI Productions. Also available are other cassette programs for personal growth and change and a workbook study course entitled: A Course In Becoming: A guide To Personal Transformation.

For the Life Mastery Catalogue of Liah Kraft-Kristaine's book and audio programs, to place an order, or to request information about Ms. Kraft-Kristaine's keynote or seminar availability, please call:

1-800-427-7982

SUGGESTED READING

LOVING RELATIONSHIPS by Sondra Ray
CREATIVE VISUALIZATION by Shakti Gawain
THE POWER OF YOUR SUBCONSCIOUS MIND by Dr.
  Joseph Murphy
THREE MAGIC WORDS by U.S. Anderson
HANDBOOK TO HIGHER CONSCIOUSNESS by Ken
  Keyes, Jr.
THE DYNAMIC LAWS OF PROSPERITY by Catherine
  Ponder
CREATING WEALTH by Robert G. Allen
PROSPERING WOMAN by Dr. Ruth Ross
THE HIPPOCRATES DIET AND HEALTH PROGRAM by
  Ann Wigmore
JET FUEL by Jeanne Jones
THE NATURE OF PERSONAL REALITY by Jane Roberts (a
  Seth book)
SETH SPEAKS by Jane Roberts
THE GATEKEEPER by Patricia Hayes
SCIENCE OF MIND by Ernest Holmes
AGARTHA by Meredith Lady Young
PASSING THE TORCH by Carol Bell Knight